Infertility
Help, Hope, and Healing

Praise for *Infertility: Help, Hope, and Healing*

"Kerstin has put a lot of thought, work, and prayer into coping with infertility. In this book, she extends her efforts to help others to cope and conquer the challenge she has so bravely faced. . . . Anyone facing any kind of health related or deeply emotional struggle will come away with a broader and deeper perspective, greater hope, and a better chance for healing in their own lives, whether their afflictions be related to infertility or other vicissitudes of the body or soul."

—James S. Heiner, MD
Founder, Reproductive Care Center,
the first private practice IVF center in Utah

"This book confirms the reality of the blessings provided by applying principles taught in the Atonement of Jesus Christ to specific individual challenges. Furthermore, it provides a resource of insight, examples, resources, and recommendations from an LDS perspective to the couple facing infertility. Kerstin's comment, 'The sting or hurt may never go away entirely, and that is normal, but we can reduce the pain to the point that it does not overwhelm us or cause us to be unproductive' describes a key benefit provided to the reader."

—C. Matthew Peterson, M.D.
John A. Dixon Presidential Professor and Chair
Department of Obstetrics and Gynecology
University of Utah Health Sciences Center

"So much of the book applies to people experiencing any type of adversity. Any reader, really, would benefit from the lessons Daynes teaches. She is sensitive, informational, and readable—all at the same time."

— Janna DeVore, Freelance Editor, Salt Lake City, UT

"Daynes effectively describes the heartache felt by those of us experiencing infertility. She offers moving recommendations from personal experience and from extensive research that both comfort the pained heart and empower the frustrated and disappointed soul."

—Jennifer Tustison, San Antonio, TX

"I can't say enough about how much I LOVE this book! Daynes has really caught the essence of struggle. It's a struggle that I still answer to every day and wonder what the right path for me will be. Daynes has an amazing understanding not only of infertility, but also of the 'balm' of the gospel."

— Susan Thiriot, Las Vegas, NV

Infertility
Help, Hope, and Healing

Kerstin Daynes

CFI
Springville, Utah

ISBN 13: 978-1-59955-296-5

Published by CFI, an imprint of Cedar Fort, Inc., 2373 W. 700 S., Springville, UT 84663
Distributed by Cedar Fort, Inc., www.cedarfort.com

LIBRARY OF CONGRESS CATALOGING-IN-PUBLICATION DATA

Daynes, Kerstin.
  Infertility : help, hope, and healing / Kerstin Daynes.
    p. cm.
  ISBN 978-1-59955-296-5
  1. Infertility--Religious aspects--Church of Jesus Christ of Latter-day
Saints. I. Title.
  RC889.D385 2009
  362.196'692--dc22
                              2009043198

Cover design by Tanya Quinlan
Cover design © 2010 by Lyle Mortimer
Edited and typeset by Melissa J. Caldwell

Printed in the United States of America

10 9 8 7 6 5 4 3 2 1

Printed on acid-free paper

I waited patiently for the lord;
and he inclined unto me, and heard my cry.
He brought me up also out of an horrible pit, out of the miry clay,
and set my feet upon a rock, and established my goings.
And he hath put a new song in my mouth, even praise unto our God:
many shall see it, and fear, and shall trust in the lord.
Blessed is that man that maketh the lord his trust.

Psalm 40:1–4

Contents

FOREWORD

⌘

Infertility is another reminder that the best of people suffer the hardest of challenges.

This book is unique in its spiritual, historical, and personal approach to the age-old problem of infertility. The reader feels less isolated when reading stories of infertility from the lives of Abraham, Isaac and Rebekah, Hannah, and Zacharias and Elisabeth. In addition, stories from ordinary and contemporary couples—and how they learned to understand and cope with the greatest challenge of their lives—bring the issue home to those living with infertility today.

This book is also unique in how it uses many treasured and utilized tools of the members of The Church of Jesus Christ of Latter-day Saints to understand and cope with the trial of infertility. Those who read this book will see that infertility is not a curse from God, but a challenge of mortal life that can be overcome by applying tried and true strategies relating to the physical, medical, emotional, mental, and social aspects of infertility. Daynes has "been there," and she has learned how to guide others through the journey. She is also sensitive to the awkward, sometimes ignorant thoughts and statements of those who have not been there, and she suggests many strategies to deal with these situations in a positive way.

Succeeding with infertility requires patience, diligence, and endurance. It requires discovering where the problems lie, accepting the reality of those problems, learning about the problems, understanding them, and learning to deal with them. It also takes understanding, strength, and hope. It requires learning to cope, adjust, and confront. It requires faith and courage. It isn't easy, and it isn't always possible to be completely successful, at least not in this lifetime. But with hope and faith come help and healing, and this book can be an important part of that process.

Infertility can be a means to learning some of the great lessons of life. In the end, infertility can usually be conquered, and it will always be a journey to be remembered.

—James S. Heiner, MD
OB/GYN, Board Certified,
Reproductive Endocrinologist, Board Certified,
Founder, Reproductive Care Center, the first private practice IVF center in Utah,
Partner, Reproductive Care Associates, Sandy, Utah

PREFACE

In December 2003, the thing I had feared for nearly five years was confirmed: I was infertile. Feelings of despair and betrayal flooded my life, and I felt isolated in my silent sorrow. As I sought help and guidance from many places, I wanted to read more about other women who knew exactly how I felt, and I wanted to make connections with those who had walked the path I was walking. In my quest, I read several books about infertility and I learned the hows, the whys, and the whats from a medical and worldly perspective. They seemed empty to me. I wanted to learn about infertility from an eternal and spiritual perspective. As I looked, I found that resources providing this spiritual strength were limited.

With the statistics showing that one out of seven couples has difficulty conceiving,[1] the number of couples in our wards, branches, and stakes that are affected by this disease is significant. As it affects so many, how could there be so little information from a Latter-day Saint perspective on the topic? Infertility is a very real disease that brings overwhelming stress, hidden losses, and associated feelings of inadequacy, sadness, and isolation.[2] I have felt all of these; but I have also learned to feel joy, strength, and power. My desire in these pages is to offer hope to you who also carry this burden. Being barren is not a guaranteed sentence to a life that is a wasteland—empty and without meaning. Your life *can* be fruitful. You *can* replenish the earth. You *can* nourish and inspire. You *can* do great things.

I wish I could address infertility from every angle or perspective and that I could entertain every possible scenario, but I cannot. Because infertility is so complex, volumes could be written about it, including the implications of infertility, scientific and medical reasons for both male and female infertility, how men and women respond differently to infertility, miscarriages and the inability to maintain pregnancies, treatment options, secondary infertility, or even how couples can better handle the situation where a pregnancy could risk the health and life of the wife. This book is only a beginning, and I truly hope it will open a door by encouraging dialogue and discussion. Although I have changed names and locations to protect identities, the situations are real. I hope it will stimulate others to share their experiences. I know that there is value in sharing our stories, our experiences, and our knowledge. Helping others understand infertility and making connections with one another can keep us from suffering alone.

Notes

1. "Infertility: An Overview—A Guide for Patients," American Society for Reproductive Medicine, 2003.
2. "Frequently Asked Questions About Infertility," http://www.asrm.org/patients/faqs.html.

Part One

HEALING YOUR SPIRIT

CHAPTER ONE

Is It Really Part of the Plan?

Like most Latter-day Saint women, I sat through six years of Young Women's lessons learning about my divine role as a woman. I made a list of every quality I wanted my husband to possess. I learned about skills that would be helpful as I became a mother. I started storing ideas—ideas I was told would be useful one day. I was told that someday I would have the sacred privilege of rearing children in the gospel and, hopefully, "teach [them] to pray, and to walk uprightly before the Lord" (D&C 68:28). I recall the excitement I felt . . . I would grow up, get married, and have children. I would find eternal happiness, just as my Young Women leaders had. Life would be exactly as I had planned—I was sure of it.

Well, I grew up, survived high school, went to college, and was married in the temple to my childhood sweetheart. Life was going just as I anticipated. Then our life together took the unexpected detour of infertility. I had never imagined that *my* life would not follow the predicted pattern. Furthermore, when life did not follow the path toward what I thought was eternal happiness, I felt betrayed by what I had been told all those years; I felt like I was being denied the blessings I was taught to expect in this mortal life. I had a hard time making sense of how my life without children could fit into the great plan of happiness, which, we all know, is about families. To me, infertility was not fair. In fact, Dr. Russell A. Foulk, said: "The system is meant to work. . . . Women are meant to get pregnant."[1]

Infertility simply does not fit our expectations of mortal life. In fact, it seems like a square peg that stubbornly resists being pounded into the round hole of the plan, no matter which way you turn the peg. How do couples live with infertility, knowing, as "The Family: A Proclamation to the World" teaches, "that the family is central to the Creator's plan for the eternal destiny of His children"?[2]

One of the things we can do to make sense of infertility is to understand the Father's plan more completely. Heavenly Father loves us as His children and wants us to have all that He has and to be with Him eternally. Heavenly Father is perfected in knowledge and body, which means He is a glorified, exalted, and eternal being. The only way that we can be with Him and to have what He has is to receive a body in this mortal life, to be resurrected through the gift of Jesus Christ, and to live a life worthy of being in His presence (also provided through Jesus Christ's Atonement and the ability to repent). That is the overall plan of Heavenly Father.

Families are an integral part of this plan because we believe the way that spirits receive bodies and enter mortality is through husbands and wives multiplying and replenishing the earth. The plan is also about our experiences in our families. Families are not just moms and dads with children, however. A family *can* be simply a husband and wife. In reality, a family *begins* with a husband and wife. A family continues through the experiences of life whether there are no children, one child, or ten children. These children grow up and move on to lives of their own, leaving the core family—husband and wife—behind. The husband and wife relationship is at the center of family life.

As I have tried to understand how infertility fits into this plan, I have found comfort in knowing that, in addition to His overall plan, Heavenly Father also has an individualized, specific plan just for me. Because I am His daughter and He knows my capabilities, talents, personality, and potential, He has created opportunities for me to learn and grow that are different from anyone else's. It is important to keep this concept of individualized micro plans in mind as we experience mortality, complete with its ups, downs, and unpredictabilities. Despite it all, our ultimate purpose here on earth is to prove ourselves worthy of living eternally with our Heavenly Father. Abraham 3:25 says, "And we will prove them herewith, to see if they will do *all* things whatsoever the Lord their God shall command them" (emphasis added). The plan is about how we keep the commandments and what we do with the experiences our Father gives us.

The Book of Mormon prophet Nephi demonstrated his personal willingness to keep the commandments and trust in his Heavenly Father. We are all familiar with the story about Nephi and his brothers being asked by Lehi (who was commanded by the Lord) to go and obtain the brass plates from Laban. Studying this well-known story more deeply can open our eyes to a greater understanding of what we can actively do to make the promises of eternity and the plan become a reality for us, regardless of our status as parents.

In 1 Nephi 3:7, Nephi says, "I will go and do the things which the Lord hath commanded, for I know that the Lord giveth no command-ments unto the children of men, save he shall prepare a way for them that they may accomplish the thing which he commandeth them."

This scripture can provide encouragement to the discouraged and downtrodden on many levels. First, we can be encouraged by under-standing that Heavenly Father has commandments, He desires for us to keep them, and He wants to bless us. In order for us to obtain those blessings, we must do our part. Can you see what our part is? We must "go" and "do." *Go* and *do* are verbs, a part of language suggesting con-scious action. We can choose our actions, meaning that we can choose to both go and do. If we choose not to "go and do the things which the Lord commanded," we cannot expect the blessings that come from com-mandment-keeping. President Gordon B. Hinckley said, "What marvel-ous things happen when men and women walk with faith in obedience to that which is required of them! . . . [I] believe that God will *always* make a way where there is no way. I believe that if we will walk in obedi-ence to the commandments of God . . . he will open a way even where there appears to be no way."[3]

What a beautiful promise, adding to the one spoken by that ancient prophet Nephi. This promise leads us into the next thing we can learn from this scripture. In the second half of the verse, Nephi promises that when the Lord gives us commandments, and we earnestly strive to keep them, He will "prepare a way for them that they may accomplish the thing which he commandeth them." Have you ever noticed that there is a footnote on the word *prepare*? Have you ever followed the footnote to the four scripture references mentioned? Until recently, I had never looked further than the page on which the scripture appears. Then I made this discovery and gained powerful wisdom from the first of the references: Genesis 18:14. It reads, "Is any thing too hard for the Lord? At the time appointed I will return unto thee, according to the time of life, and Sarah shall have a son." Who knew that this scripture in 1 Nephi could have anything to do with infertility? It is not *all* about infertility, of course, but it does gives us insight that can change our perspective.

We learn that nothing is too hard for the Lord. We learn that He is very aware of our lives, our sorrows, and our pains. We learn that because Heavenly Father has commanded us to "multiply, and replenish the earth" (Moses 2:28), He will *prepare* a way if we "go" and "do" our part. This promise does not specify a when or a how, but it does say that He will prepare and provide. He may not grant us the ability to multiply and replenish the earth by conceiving and bearing children, but He will provide us with opportunities to multiply and replenish in other spheres of our lives. Elder Richard G. Scott said, "I testify that when the Lord closes one important door in your life, He shows His continuing love and compassion by opening many other compensating doors through your exercise of faith."[4]

As we are faithful, our lives and hearts change, our perspective changes, and our vision expands. Faithful living changes the way we live and think, the way we trust our Heavenly Father, and the way we believe, until, as Sister Ardeth G. Kapp taught, "We realize that the tests we are called upon to endure are for our growth, not to consume us but to refine us, not to discourage us but to enlighten us, and not to defeat us but to redeem us."[5]

The result is we see from the beginning that infertility does fit into the plan. It is the part of the plan called adversity, which was presented in the premortal existence. Adversity is part of the exalting process, the process of making us worthy to be gods and goddesses and to live with Heavenly Father eternally—that is the eternal happiness my Young Women leaders taught me about many years ago.

Bishop Richard C. Edgley described so clearly how we each accepted the plan, complete with adversities, with focused spiritual eyes:

> I believe we all understood that by coming to earth, we would be exposed to all of the experiences of earth life, including the not-so-pleasant trials. . . . There would be opposition and adversity. And if that was all we knew about the plan, I doubt if any of us would have embraced it, rejoicing, "That's what I have always wanted—pain, suffering, hopelessness, sin, and death." But it all came into focus, and it became acceptable, even desirable, when an Elder Brother stepped forward and offered that He would go down and make it all right. Out of pain and suffering He would bring peace. Out of hopelessness He would bring hope. Out of transgression He would bring repentance and forgiveness. Out of death He would bring the resurrection of lives. And with that explanation and most generous offer, each and every one of us concluded, "I can do that. That is a risk worth taking." And so we chose.[6]

So, the "more easily said than done" answer is to strive to obtain those eyes we once saw with when we perceived eternally. Then we will be more likely to see infertility as it fits into the wider scope of eternity. We do not have to try to alter it or massage it in order for it to fit. Rather, accepting it as our own refiner's fire and recognizing that it can be instrumental in preparing us to meet our Heavenly Father allows us to begin to endure. With focused spiritual labor, we can fortify our faith and seek understanding so that our vision today can be as clear "as it was when we first made that choice, . . . [and that] we would choose again."[7]

As we work toward this enhanced perspective, we will recognize that Heavenly Father provides ways for us to accomplish those things which He wants and needs us to do. And, all the while, He will provide a way for us to be who He sees we can become, regardless of our status as a mother or father. Remember that life *can* be fruitful despite circumstance. And we *can* replenish the earth by filling it with good and righteous things. It is important to stop judging ourselves and our lives based upon a perceived better plan that has been created by expectations. As we are living righteously and obediently, the best plan for us is the one we are living.

My Young Women leaders were right. My life *is* on the path toward eternal happiness, and I *can* receive the blessings Heavenly Father has made available to me. Things have turned out differently than I expected, but it has been the difference that has tutored me. It has been exactly what I need in order to find happiness and to recognize that Heavenly Father indeed has prepared a way for me to fulfill those very things He has planned for me, His daughter. As I "go and do" by demonstrating my personal willingness to trust Him and to keep all of His command-ments, I will see my soul expand, my heart purified, and my life become enriched with purpose and meaning.

Notes

1. "Common Obstacles to IVF Success," In*focus*, Fall 2003, 9.
2. "The Family: A Proclamation to the World," *Ensign*, Nov. 1995, 102.
3. Gordon B. Hinckley, "If Ye Be Willing and Obedient," *Ensign*, July 1995, 2; emphasis added.
4. Richard G. Scott, "Trust in the Lord," *Ensign*, Nov. 1995, 17.
5. Ardeth G. Kapp, *My Neighbor, My Sister, My Friend* (Salt Lake City: Deseret Book, 1990), ix.
6. Richard C. Edgley, "For Thy Good," *Ensign*, May 2002, 65.
7. Ibid.

CHAPTER TWO

Judge Him Faithful Who Promised

President Henry B. Eyring has taught that the scriptures are "a way for God to reveal things to [us] that are personal and helpful."[1]

These ancient writings not only provide answers to life's experiences, but they also give depth to our perspective and understanding. For this reason, let's look at several scripture stories about faithful women who knew firsthand the feelings associated with infertility. These women lived righteous lives, exercised extreme faith, and "waited patiently for the Lord" (Psalm 40:1). Their persistence in doing what was right is noteworthy. After all, they persisted for many years, decades, and in some cases, an entire lifetime. Elder Neal A. Maxwell said, "Sometimes that which we are doing is correct enough but simply needs to be persisted in patiently, not for a minute or a moment but sometimes for years. Paul speaks of the marathon of life and of how we must 'run with patience the race that is set before us' (Hebrews 12:1). Paul did not select the hundred-meter dash for his analogy!"[2]

Paul also did not counsel us to walk gingerly through the experiences of life; rather, he said to run, suggesting vigor and effort. What picture does that conjure up in your mind?

I imagine these scriptural heroines running with all of their might with unwavering faith and without doubt, continuing "in the things which [they had] learned and [had] been assured of" (2 Timothy 3:14). Ultimately— in the twilight of life for some—they "judged him faithful who had promised" (Hebrews 11:11). Together, we can gain wisdom and hope from these miraculous stories—they have become sweet companions to me.

Sarah

The story of Sarah and her husband, Abraham, is well-known. Sarah was married to a prophet of God (a prophet of God who was promised some very specific blessings). I imagine that life for this Old Testament family was in many ways rather ordinary—some days were joyful and others were challenging. In Genesis, we learn that Haran, Abraham's brother, died at a young age. Haran had a son—the infamous Lot. Upon Haran's death, Lot became the responsibility of Abraham's father, Terah. Together with Abraham and Sarah, both Terah and Lot traveled to a new land. Terah died in this new land, leaving Lot with Abraham and Sarah.

As we can see, this family had a taste of adversity on many levels—the deaths of two family members, adjusting to a new community, and adapting to a mixed-family situation. And, as is common, the adversity did not end there. This family endured another move to Canaan, a famine, the anger of Pharaoh, and the overwhelming disappointment of Lot's choice to separate himself from the family, leading to the experiences in Sodom and Gomorrah. Not to be overshadowed by these misfortunes, Sarah was barren and had been for many years.

Abraham's name means "father of a multitude,"[3] which seems extraordinarily ironic, seeing that he married Sarah, who "was barren; she had no child" (Genesis 11:30). I wonder how Sarah felt since she knew of her barrenness, was required to help care for Lot, and then learned that Heavenly Father's plan for her husband included seed without number. I wonder if she held on to that plan as a promise that she would be a mother, or if she felt inadequate knowing that physically she could not fulfill that plan. How often did Sarah wonder how her barrenness would fit in this scenerio? Were Sarah's yearnings to mother a child fulfilled as she cared for Lot?

The Lord continually reminded Abraham of the plan He had for him: "Unto thy seed will I give this land" (Genesis 12:7), and "I will make thy seed as the dust of the earth: so that if a man can number the dust of the earth, then shall thy seed also be numbered" (Genesis 13:16), and "I will make thee exceeding fruitful" (Genesis 17:6). I would guess that after repeatedly hearing about these promises and the plan, Abraham and Sarah probably wondered how it could possibly be fulfilled.

The Lord appeared to Abraham in a vision during which Abraham took the opportunity to clarify a few things. He said to the Lord, "Behold, to me thou hast given no seed: and, lo, one born in my house is mine heir," speaking of Eliezer of Damascus, a steward of his house.

The Lord replied by saying, "This shall not be thine heir; but he that shall come forth out of thine own bowels shall be thine heir. . . . Look now toward heaven, and tell the stars, if thou be able to number them: . . . So shall thy seed be." I am sure Abraham was confused as to how exactly this promise would be fulfilled; however, he trusted. The scriptures say, "And he believed in the Lord; and he counted it to him for righteousness" (Genesis 15:3–6).

Even after this spiritual exchange with the Lord, Abraham and Sarah did not see a fulfillment of the promise. Sarah gave Hagar (her handmaiden) to Abraham to wife, according to the law (see D&C 132:34). I wonder how intense the turmoil must have been for Sarah at this time. Perhaps she might have thought, "So, the Lord has denied me the very thing He promised. And now I have to live with the fact that my husband's children—the ones who will inherit many great things—will be with another woman."

As Hagar had a son, Sarah continued longing. Abraham and Sarah were old, and "well stricken in age," and the hope for children was fading (see Genesis 18:11). Then, after many years of tribulation, patience, prayer, and faith, there was a glimmer of hope. The Lord said to Abraham, "And I will bless [Sarah], and give thee a son also of her: yea, I will bless her, and she shall be a mother of nations; kings of people shall be of her" (Genesis 17:16).

I appreciate the responses of these two faithful servants—they were human indeed. "Abraham fell upon his face, and laughed, and said in his heart, Shall a child be born unto him that is an hundred years old? and shall Sarah, that is ninety years old, bear? . . . And God said, Sarah thy wife shall bear thee a son indeed; and thou shalt call his name Isaac: and I will establish my covenant with him" (Genesis 17:17, 19).

After many years of being reminded of the promise, Abraham's reaction is one of "Sure, now, when we are old and feeble, we will have a son." Sarah's reaction was very similar: "Therefore Sarah laughed within herself, saying, After I am waxed old shall I have pleasure?" To which the Lord responded, "Is any thing too hard for the Lord? At the time appointed I will return unto thee, according to the time of life, and Sarah shall have a son" (Genesis 18:12, 14). In Genesis 17:17, the footnote for the word *laughed* lists a second meaning: *rejoiced*. Imagine the great disbelief *and* joy they must have experienced as husband and wife on that day.

In his dissertation on faith to the Hebrews, Paul the Apostle mentions the extraordinary faith of Sarah. "Through faith also Sara herself received strength to conceive seed, and was delivered of a child when she was past age, because she judged him faithful who had promised" (Hebrews 11:11).

I love this message! In this scripture, the word *judged* implies that Sarah trusted that the Lord would be faithful to His promises, and she was determined to hold Him to those promises. Abraham and Sarah remained faithful, keeping covenants and establishing a legacy of extraordinary faith. The Lord had a unique plan for this family, one that was different than the normal "grow up, get married, have children, and live happily ever after" plan. The plan that He had for Abraham and Sarah included all of the things He had promised, but they happened at a different time than they expected. In the end, they experienced joy, perhaps more exquisite because of their patience, faith, and "judging him faithful who had promised." In the Joseph Smith Translation of Hebrews 11:40, which speaks of people who had suffered many afflictions, it states, "God having provided some better things for them through their sufferings, for without sufferings they could not be made perfect." We are truly made more perfect, more like our Father in Heaven, and more ready for salvation through our trials—even the trial of infertility.

Hannah

Hannah was one of the two wives of Elkanah. Elkanah's other wife, Peninnah, had children, but Hannah was barren. Every year, the entire family went to the tabernacle to offer sacrifice. As was customary, a portion of the sacrificial animal was returned to the one who offered it to be used in a special feast. "From his part, Elkanah gave portions of the meat to his family. Hannah received either more than the others or else a more choice portion because of Elkanah's love for her."[4]

There were apparently some sore feelings between Peninnah and Hannah. Perhaps Peninnah was jealous of Hannah because Elkanah loved Hannah so deeply; so deeply, in fact, that he gave her a greater or more choice portion of the sacrificial animal every year. Peninnah continually "provoked" Hannah and tried "to make her fret" (1 Samuel 1:6) because the Lord had left her barren. Year after year this tension was made worse at the time of sacrifice when "Peninnah took this opportunity particularly to twit Hannah with her barrenness, by making an ostentatious exhibition of her children."[5] Peninnah was successful in her plight because these actions caused Hannah great distress. Hannah would weep and refuse food.

Hannah went to the temple and took her heavy, bitter, and sorrowing heart to the Lord. She prayed and vowed that "if thou wilt indeed look on the affliction of thine handmaid, and remember me, and not forget thine handmaid, but wilt give unto thine handmaid a man child, then I will give him unto the Lord all the days of his life" (1 Samuel 1:11). Hannah was not alone in the temple that day. Eli, a priest, heard Hannah's prayer and said, "Go in peace: and the God of Israel grant thee thy petition that thou hast asked of him" (1 Samuel 1:17). Hannah left, went to eat, and "her countenance was no more sad" (1 Samuel 1:18). A very short time later, Hannah did conceive—the Lord had remembered her. She had a son and called him Samuel, meaning "heard of God," as a reminder to both Hannah and Samuel of the miracle surrounding his birth.[6] Once Samuel was weaned, she took him to the tabernacle where "as long as he liveth he shall be lent to the Lord" (1 Samuel 1:28).

Even though Hannah did not know how her barrenness fit into the plan, nor did she know when or how the desires of her heart would be granted, she trusted that the promises made to her would be kept. As she trusted and had faith, she was granted strength to endure her suffering, even such that her countenance changed. Through her faith, and according to His will, the Lord gave Hannah the power to conceive and bear a child. She then fulfilled her part of the promise and gave her son to the work of the Lord.

Elisabeth

Elisabeth was another faithful scriptural heroine. She was a relative of Mary, the mother of Jesus. Elisabeth was married to Zacharias who was a priest and served in the temple. Both Zacharias and Elisabeth were said to be "righteous before God, walking in all the commandments and ordinances of the Lord blameless" (Luke 1:6). Elisabeth was barren, and when we enter their story, as depicted in the Gospel of Luke, they were not getting any younger; in fact, "they both were now well stricken in years" (Luke 1:7).

Without a doubt, their barrenness was difficult on both Zacharias and Elisabeth, and I am sure it was on their minds more often than not. One day, as Zacharias was attending to his responsibility of burning incense in the temple, an angel appeared to him. It was the time of incense, which meant that there was likely a multitude of people outside the temple. When the angel appeared, Zacharias became fearful and troubled, as many of us might be if an angel appeared to us. The angel spoke to him saying, "Fear not, Zacharias: for thy prayer is heard; and thy wife Elisabeth shall bear thee a son, and thou shalt call his name John" (Luke 1:13). I cannot imagine that this was the first time Zacharias prayed about this particular struggle. I believe that Zacharias and Elisabeth had prayed countless times about this over the previous decades, both individually and as a couple. So, why did it take so long for the prayer to be answered?

As the angel continued to visit with Zacharias, the angel revealed that "Thou shalt have joy and gladness; and many shall rejoice at his birth" (what an understatement!). Zacharias's promised son had a specific mission and individualized plan to fulfill for the Lord; after all, the angel said, "many shall rejoice at his birth. For he shall be great in the sight of the Lord" (Luke 1:14–15). Zacharias would not live to see this prophecy come to fruition, but John would be strictly obedient, have the gift of the Holy Ghost, prepare the way for the Lord, and be a missionary that would help "many of the children of Israel . . . turn to the Lord their God" (Luke 1:16).

Zacharias doubted and questioned this new plan from Heavenly Father. I think I probably would have too. After many years of constant prayer and much faith, how could he be assured that it would really happen? He asked the angel, "Whereby shall I know this? for I am an old man, and my wife well stricken in years" (Luke 1:18). The angel told him that he had been in the presence of God and was sent to tell Zacharias this wonderful news. Because of his disbelief, Zacharias was struck dumb. The angel told him that he would not be able to speak until the day of John's birth.

As the story goes, Elisabeth conceived; Heavenly Father took "away [her] reproach among men" (Luke 1:25). Remember, childbearing was an honor for women (and it remains so in our day) and an expectation of society during biblical times because within a woman was the possibility of posterity. When a woman could not conceive, society disapproved of her—she was a disappointment and brought shame upon her family. I can imagine that many criticized these women, including family, friends, and the community—thus having "reproach among men." I think we see this in some cases in our day. Couples who have been married for a long time and are childless are judged by some. Some people see these couples as selfish for not having children, when in reality it may be their greatest desire—something far from selfish.

You may recall that while Elisabeth was pregnant, the miracle of Mary's conception occurred. The angel who visited Mary was the same angel who visited Zacharias. This angel not only told Mary that she would bear a child and call him Jesus, he also told Mary of Elisabeth's miraculous conception. He told her that "with God nothing shall be impossible" (Luke 1:37), a comment associated directly with Elisabeth's miracle.

As prophesied by the angel, when Elisabeth delivered, her neighbors and relatives rejoiced with her. Once Zacharias's speech was returned, he too praised God. I can see families today celebrating and rejoicing when a daughter and her husband, son and his wife, sister and her husband, or friend has a child after a period of great anticipation. It is a time of joy and a time to praise God, for He has heard and answered the prayers of many.

The story of John was "noised abroad. . . . And all they that heard them laid them up in their hearts, saying, What manner of child shall this be!" Zacharias said, "Thou, child, shalt be called the prophet of the Highest: for thou shalt go before the face of the Lord to prepare his ways;

to give knowledge of salvation unto his people by the remission of their sins, through the tender mercy of our God; . . . to give light to them that sit in darkness and in the shadow of death, to guide our feet into the way of peace" (Luke 1:65–66, 76–79).

John did indeed have a special purpose. Heavenly Father needed him at a certain time, in a certain place, and born to certain parents. Had he fulfilled Elisabeth and Zacharias's hopes according to their desired time-table, John would not have been able to fulfill God's purpose and plan. John grew and gained spiritual strength. He was a remarkable mission-ary, fulfilled many prophesies, and truly prepared the way for Christ. He baptized Jesus Christ, bore a powerful testimony of Him, and died an unwavering disciple.

I can visualize each of these biblical couples as they exercised faith and sought for miracles. I can see them kneeling together and separately, humbly praying with all the energy of their souls, pleading with their Father in Heaven. I can see them fasting, not only on "fast Sunday," but often, demonstrating their desire to put their will into compliance with Heavenly Father's. I can see them seeking the direction of the Spirit so they would have comfort, strength, and peace upon them. I can see them faithfully serving, doing good things in their communities, and living their lives in harmony with the things they knew were right.

I am sure they all had their moments of anger, bitterness, question-ing, and doubt. They were human—as we are. They were not perfect. Remember Abraham's doubts as he questioned the Lord regarding how His promises could be fulfilled? How about Hannah's deep sorrow and her refusal to eat when they had their sacrificial feast? And remember Zacharias's inability to simply trust the words of an angel?

They may have reached the point of admitting that they would never have children. After all, each couple had been married for many years with no success with conception. They may have felt there was no more hope. I would not be surprised if Sarah wondered what was wrong with her because she could not perform one of the most basic and important tasks of womanhood. I would guess that Elisabeth would have welcomed the assistance of a reproductive endocrinologist. I would imagine that each felt she had failed her husband in some way. Being a woman who knows the sorrow, I know that each of them, with their husbands, cried each month when yet again, they were denied a child. I can also see the joy they must have felt when their prayers were answered and they were granted the very desires of their hearts. I am sure that both husband and wife rejoiced and praised the Father for His long-awaited generosity.

Abraham and Sarah, Elkanah and Hannah, Zacharias and Elisabeth—each of them longed, and each of them sorrowed. They all prayed and had faith for many years. They were all blessed. They all saw miracles wrought in their lives.

"Has the day of miracles ceased? Or have angels ceased to appear unto the children of men? Or has he withheld the power of the Holy Ghost from them? . . . Behold I say unto you, Nay; for it is by faith that miracles are wrought; and it is by faith that angels appear and minister unto men; wherefore, if these things have ceased wo be unto the children of men, for it is because of unbelief, and all is vain" (Moroni 7:35–37).

I read this scripture on January 19, 2004, not long after I found out my prognosis. Next to that verse, I wrote in my scriptures: "We need a miracle."

Notes

1. Henry B. Eyring, "A Discussion on Scripture Study," *Ensign*, July 2005, 22.
2. Neal A. Maxwell, "Patience," in *1979 Devotional Speeches of the Year* (Provo, UT: Brigham Young University Press, 1980), 216.
3. Bible Dictionary, "Abraham," 601.
4. *Old Testament Student Manual, Genesis—2 Samuel* (Salt Lake City: The Church of Jesus Christ of Latter-day Saints, 2003), 267.
5. Ibid.
6. Ibid., 268.

CHAPTER THREE

⌾⌾⌾

...But Do Miracles Always Happen?

Each of the scriptural stories reviewed in the previous chapter had the same resolution: the miracle of conception, pregnancy, and birth. Certainly, this is what every infertile couple hopes for. Some infertile women *will* receive the miracle of life within their wombs; however, others—despite continued faithfulness and heartfelt pleading—will not. If the miracle of conception is not granted, it is easy to feel that you are unworthy or that you have not found favor in the sight of God. How is it possible to "[judge] him faithful who had promised" (Hebrews 11:11) when the miracle we expect does not happen? It can certainly feel as though miracles have ceased.

May I suggest exploring the meaning of a miracle? I think most of us hear the word *miracle* and think of the miracles experienced by Sarah, Hannah, and Elisabeth—conceiving when all hope seemed lost. Or perhaps you think of Jairus's daughter being raised from the dead or of the Red Sea being parted so that the Israelites could cross on dry ground. These events were, indeed, extraordinary miracles.

But the works of God do not need to equal the parting of the Red Sea to be considered miracles. A miracle can be simple. A miracle can be a family that consciously chooses to begin having family home evening together or a marriage relationship being strengthened by a commitment of selflessness. Miracles of this sort happen each day. And while the "big" miracles we expect or desire may not happen, the miracles that Heavenly Father knows we need *always* happen.

Sister Susan W. Tanner, previous general president of the Young Women, said, "As I read the stories of Jesus' Apostles after His death, I see that they were frequently and brutally persecuted, stoned, and imprisoned. But they lived with courage and faith. They knew that ultimately all things would work together for their good. They also knew that through interim blessings and miracles, things were working out. They were sustained, tutored, and protected. They embraced the promises not only afar off but here and now as well."[1]

As with the Apostles of old, we who experience a trial such as infertility can also know through interim blessings and miracles that things are working together for our good. These small and simple miracles can give us courage and can sustain us. They will help to enlarge our belief in Heavenly Father's power, and our faith will be encouraged. These miracles also help us to know that our faithful ways are not in vain and that Heavenly Father recognizes every effort we make to do what He asks. Miracles in our lives become obvious as we focus our eyes through searching, praying, and believing.

It is important to remember, as Elder Dallin H. Oaks taught, that "the will of the Lord is always paramount"; we cannot change His will.[2] We can, however, change ours. This change is undoubtedly a very difficult task, requiring much time on bended knee and in spiritual meditation. But in the end, aligning our will to Heavenly Father's is a miracle in and of itself and will bless our lives beyond measure.

How do miracles happen? Miracles "are a response to faith. . . . They [are] never wrought without prayer, felt need, and faith."[3] They will happen in the Lord's time and in the Lord's way. We should not suppose that we can determine the schedule of our Heavenly Father; after all, He is the One with a perfect and eternal perspective and can see the end from the beginning. As hard as it is to admit, we can only control the choices we make, and those choices determine the lives that we live. We can choose to live a faith-filled life regardless of the ups and downs we encounter. Remember, miracles will cease only when faith has ceased.

We all know women who are seeking for the miracle of conception, pregnancy, and birth. Additionally, we all know that it can be painful as we see women around us receiving this miracle, while we try to wait patiently. Some women are at the beginning of their quest for children, while others are seasoned by years of sadness without them. What is comforting is that many women are choosing to live faithful lives and to accept the will of Heavenly Father. As they 'judge Him faithful,' unexpected miracles are being made manifest in their lives. Let us learn from some of them.

Maren and Chris

Let me tell you about Maren and her husband, Chris. They were married in 2001 in the Denver Colorado Temple. As many couples do before they get married, Maren and Chris spent time discussing what they wanted out of life. Among the things they talked about were education, spirituality, places to live, and, of course, having a family. They were confident about their plans and that Heavenly Father was pleased with the path they were choosing. After 1½ years of marriage, however, they began to be concerned about their plan to have children. Maren was not getting pregnant.

Imagine this: they were students at BYU in Provo, Utah, and living in Wymount (married student housing). Every student at BYU could present you with a carefully crafted list of the rumors surrounding this complex: "they are like rabbit hutches," "it has been proven that breathing on each other causes conception," or "you won't leave Wymount without having children." Maren and Chris were the exception in this Fertile City, however, and (secretly) so are many others.

They decided to approach their OB/GYN and begin their quest to find answers. Various tests were performed, numerous procedures tried, and potential problems ruled out. Tears were spilt, plans and dreams frustrated, and a measure of hope lost. Years have passed since their first disappointments, and they are still without a diagnosis and a prognosis.

People are baffled when they find out that Maren and Chris aren't newlyweds. The unfair assumption is made that they must be in the first years of marriage simply because they are childless. The real reason they are childless is beyond their control. In their seemingly endless quest for answers, they often wonder if they should continue with procedures since there is no true guarantee once they have invested their time, money, and emotions. The reason for their infertility may be irreparable or even untreatable, and pregnancy may be something they will never know. But they, like many couples, believe that if they had answers, their focus and perspective could change and they could begin dealing with their infertility in a different way.

Maren knows the betrayal that comes month after month, test after test, and procedure after procedure. She has felt the loss of hope when each doctor cannot fix her problem because he cannot even determine what it is. She has experienced frustration when she hears of those with children complain about them or treat them disrespectfully. She has seen day-to-day choices as well as long-term plans impacted by her infertility. She has felt inadequate. She has wondered what her life is supposed to be. And she has cried a multitude of tears as she has considered the thought that she may never have an answer and that she may never have a child.

As with most infertile women, Maren has felt that years of sincere prayers have gone unanswered, concluding that it surely must be because she has forgotten to live one of the commandments. Over time, however, her testimony and her love for the Gospel have reshaped and nurtured a new perspective. "The gospel gives me hope," she says, "and a sense of where to turn. I know that I can turn to my Savior by praying and reading my scriptures. I have learned to change my prayers so they are more meaningful. I now pray for more than to just have a baby—I pray for direction. It certainly isn't easy, but I know where to go." Maren continues, "As I have learned more about the gospel, I know that my infertility is not caused by unrighteousness. I have also learned that I can't just dwell on the commandment to multiply and replenish the earth. Even if I can't physically multiply and replenish the earth, my intentions can still be there and I will be blessed."

In an effort to show Heavenly Father that her intentions are right and that she is doing all within her power, she is working at strengthening her relationship with Him and her Savior, Jesus Christ. Even though each day is not a spiritual high, she does see this relationship evolving and her eyes have been opened to the blessings that are helping her to trust Heavenly Father. "I am continually developing my trust in Him," Maren says. "I am coming to understand that there isn't just one way for things to happen. I am learning to believe that there is a plan for me specifically and that to Him, there is a reason that I am experiencing infertility."

As Maren and I spoke, she began to notice that even in the darkest of times, there are gentle reminders that Heavenly Father is aware of her as well as her desires. She is beginning to acknowledge them as miracles. Let me share some of them with you.

After finishing his Masters in Public Administration at BYU, Chris accepted a job with the city of Palo Alto, California. They headed into the great unknown by moving hundreds of miles away from both families. Additionally, Maren left a financially and professionally profitable career with an insurance company and did not know what she would do to fill her time.

Once they were semi-settled in a new environment, Maren set out to find a job. She accepted a "work-from-home" data entry position thinking it would be easy and convenient. It was something but was not what she wanted. Her life's dream was not to work, but rather to be a mother. The undesirable parts of this new job only intensified the frustration of having to conform to a different plan. She prayed earnestly for direction, feeling that she desperately needed guidance to adapt to this different plan. Her answer came in an unexpected way.

When Maren received her visiting teaching assignment in her new ward, she learned that her companion was an eighty-year-old sister. How different! Looking back on her short list of previous companions, she noted that they were all young, usually newly married, and in similar life experiences as herself. This sister did not fit that description in any way.

She went with her companion on a visit for the first time. As is common, the first visit was about getting to know one another and sharing about families, jobs, and so forth. So, the topic of Maren's job came up. Fulfilling her part in the conversation, she explained what she did, that it was not particularly fulfilling, and that she was continuing to look for something different. A few weeks after the visit, her companion's husband called with a job opportunity, and Maren accepted it. This new job transformed Maren's life. The job gave Maren an excuse to leave her house, to have a change of pace, to converse with other people, and to use her skills. Because of her hard work, she quickly moved into a supervisory role. The job was low stress, flexible, gave her unique responsibilities, and she loved it. She felt successful, and she belonged!

Maren knows that this eighty-year-old visiting teaching companion was not coincidental. Heavenly Father knew what she needed, when she needed it, and knew the best way to deliver it to her. Note that she did her part too. She prayed earnestly, had faith that all things would work together for her good, and went to work. In time, she became close friends with her boss who knew the pains of infertility firsthand. They could share feelings of concern and understanding, particularly as they went through tests and procedures. That is another miracle—an understanding friend!

Palo Alto was providing Maren with other miracles. First, she was no longer surrounded by twenty-year-olds having babies. It *was* acceptable to be twenty-five and without children! Yes, her dream of becoming a mother was still very present in her mind, but she did not feel that she was constantly being judged because she did not have children. Additionally, Palo Alto did not just change her location; it somehow created an ability to deal with her emotions differently. She still cried the same tears every month when she found out she was not pregnant, and she still felt intense sorrow. But Palo Alto was a fresh start, which empowered her to take control of those feelings of sadness and to begin feeling more accustomed to her infertility.

Through her struggle with infertility, Maren also felt she has been prepared to help others and to be a comforting influence. She has moved away from thinking that she is the only one who is suffering and acknowledges that everyone experiences times of being stretched spiritually and being overwhelmed with the accompanying emotions. "Even though I do forget sometimes and become selfish," she says, "I have become more sensitive to the feelings of others." Because she has been hurt by well-meaning yet insensitive comments from others, she has resolved to be more compassionate and respectful to others during their suffering. Additionally, she believes that "we may have people cross our path now or many years from now who we will be able to understand because of a trial we had." She sees that the not-so-gentle spiritual stretching of this trial is molding her into what Heavenly Father needs and wants her to become—Christlike and "more fit for the kingdom."[4] Another miracle.

Comfort at unexpected times has also been a miracle in Maren's life. Even on the worst days—the ones filled with the greatest discouragement—she prays. She admits, "It is often hard to pray . . . but some of the most wonderful times have been on my knees praying for help. I have felt the comfort come at random times . . . at these moments, everything seems okay." Many of us can relate to feeling encircled by comfort and peace while on bended knees. If the blessings of prayer are truly so deep, eternal, and satisfying, why do we not pray more or with greater intent? And how can we preserve these feelings of strength and consolation as these prayerful moments draw to a close?

Maren has also discovered her ability to process feelings differently. She attributes this maturity to observing and talking to others, as well as receiving knowledge and promptings from the Spirit. For example, she used to be convinced that if she had children, she would surely be happy and complete. This way of thinking caused her to diminish or overlook some of the greatest blessings from a loving Heavenly Father. Even though rejoicing about her infertility is an impossibility, she is learning to find happiness with her life as it is now. Reserving happiness for the future causes the moment to lose its meaning, depth, and purpose. Besides, no one can be confident that children will bring desired happiness, fill every void, and solve problems. Instead, children will present a whole new set of challenges and certainly not provide happiness every day. Maren is striving to find happiness in the present. Yes, a miracle!

The list of miracles goes on, including Maren's relationship with her husband—it has deepened as they have learned to work together, to understand each other's feelings, to communicate more effectively about their infertility, and as they have adjusted their life goals to accommodate this change in their plan. Feelings of gratitude have surfaced as Maren has seen blessings in such things as opportunities to share her experiences and feelings with others; having infertile friends who understand exactly what she is going through; being able to rely on a sister-in-law who has compassionately cried tears with her; and trusting a sister who also experiences infertility. None of these small miracles are coincidental. They are interim blessings that, once detected, have helped sustained Maren, encouraging her, lifting her, and giving her spiritual momentum.

Brad and Megan

When diagnosed with infertility, my friend Megan considered it one more thing to be heaped upon the already mounting problems that seemed out of her control.

She and Brad had been married for quite some time, and it had become apparent that they had very different goals concerning a family. Hers? Starting now. His? Starting later. Over time, they decided that because of these differing perspectives and the conflict they caused, the topic was better avoided altogether. They were strained both individually and as a couple. They even considered separating. They bounced between their bishop and a professional counselor, trying to understand each other and mend many hurt feelings. Together with their bishop, Megan and Brad realigned priorities and began to work toward having a family. Then came the suspicions of infertility.

When I say that infertility affects the marriage relationship, I know I state the obvious; emotions, opinions, and decisions add stress that no one really wants to deal with. For Brad and Megan, the stresses of infertility were now being added to a marriage where stress had already been accumulating for years. Megan felt that beginning the quest to understand their infertility and to hopefully conceive was the next step in their newly determined goal to start a family. Brad was not so sure. Yes, he had agreed to begin a family, but seeking answers to their infertility was not something he wanted to entertain. So, alone, Megan sought help. Alone, Megan was tested. And alone, Megan underwent treatments.

Megan spent long months on Clomid (a medication that stimulates ovulation), hoping each month would bring success. She was discouraged that nothing was working, that her options were running out, and that her husband refused to be tested. Infertility options and treatment can hit a dead-end pretty quickly without the support and involvement of a spouse. Despite pleas from Megan, Brad would not be tested, nor would he go to appointments with her; in fact, it was simply easier to go alone rather than deal with the fight or stress of trying to persuade him to go. Even though she felt frustrated and lonely, her only option was to continue to pray. She prayed for guidance and direction, but most of all, she prayed that her husband's heart would soften.

After many months of prayer and continuing treatments on her own, Megan learned that Brad was unsure of the Church's perspective on infertility, both testing and treatments. He emphasized that he was committed to not doing anything that would be against the beliefs of the Church or compromising his standing in the Church, which, of course, Megan appreciated. Megan had finally found a reason for his resistance! Learning about the cause of her husband's uncertainty was not only a breakthrough—it was an answer to heartfelt prayers. Megan knew just what to do: go to the bishop. In a phone call, Megan described the problem to her bishop and asked for guidance. The bishop quoted the Church's policies regarding infertility testing and procedures. Megan then passed this information on to Brad.

Slowly, things began to change. Even though it wasn't the next day or even the following week, change began with Brad agreeing to be tested. When the results came back, they found out that he was, indeed, part of their infertility problem. Brad was shocked, unsure of what to think, and he did not know how to respond to the fact that he was part of the problem. In fact, he did not want to talk about it at all. Together, Brad and Megan were disappointed and felt that these results only added to the list of challenges they had to resolve. As they allowed the news to settle, however, they saw that with this diagnosis, they also had answers they did not have before. With these answers, they knew that their only options for conceiving would be artificial insemination (AI) or in vitro fertilization (IVF). They no longer had to deal with the uncertainty of wondering which treatments to consider.

As Brad and Megan pursued AI, their relationship began to change. They were communicating more openly and honestly. Even though it still involved powerful convincing to get Brad to participate in the procedures, Megan was thrilled that Brad was beginning to accept the process and becoming more compliant. He even started talking more about children!

Brad and Megan continued to experience disappointments month after month. With the frustration of procedures failing, the stress of procedures not being covered by insurance, and the loss of privacy, hope of becoming parents did not improve. Along with every failure, Megan shed tears of sorrow, betrayal, and frustration. Each month increased her doubt that anything would work. While Megan was upset, Brad seemed unaffected or unbothered about the failures. He did not know how to make Megan feel better nor did he know what to do or say. As she experienced these feelings of deep sadness, Megan began to recognize that because of their differing perspectives, wanting Brad to feel the same way when procedures failed was unreasonable. They began to communicate about ways to comfort and strengthen each other during these trying times. While Megan needed extra love and attention during the grieving following failures, Brad needed respect and patience as he adapted to his diagnosis and his role in treatments and procedures.

In the moments when she wondered what she did to deserve the struggles in her marriage, infertility, and the frustrating reluctance of her husband, unique and specific blessings were becoming evident in Megan's life. Megan saw that the process of trial was indeed encouraging her relationship with her husband to evolve into one of unity and love. They were learning to work together and to communicate. Megan began to see that having a baby in the early days of their marriage probably would have destroyed them and that perhaps the change in their relationship needed to occur before they had children. Perhaps it was a tempering or preparation—timing is everything.

Brad's receptiveness to testing and procedures was another obvious blessing and could be counted as a miracle. Not only did this change in her husband strengthen Megan's faith in prayer, it confirmed to Megan that she was not alone in her quest for children and that she and her husband finally had the same goal. In the quiet moments when Brad would pray that they would be able to have children, Megan's heart was warmed and her hope increased. She was overwhelmingly grateful for the transformation she had witnessed. She knew she had received an incredible gift from a loving Heavenly Father and knew that He was aware of her and her specific needs.

During the hardest times, Megan received unique, interim blessings in the form of love from her family. As her parents offered listening ears, Megan found acceptance and hope. Additionally, she found unexpected, yet welcomed, comfort from Brad's grandmother. His grandmother seemed unusually educated about infertility as well as its associated treatments and procedures, thus she was able to provide nonjudgmental encouragement and knew just what to say. She proved to be genuinely concerned about the process they were going through and became a great blessing.

As she endured the unpredictability and pains of infertility, Megan found happiness in giving much needed love and attention to her niece, Sophie. Sophie's home life was not particularly stable or happy, and because of circumstance, Megan provided positive experiences for her. Sophie filled a deep void in Megan's life. Additionally, Megan shared her skills to nurture those who needed love by working in the nursing profession. Although the hours were unusual, she has had very rewarding and life-altering experiences that have shown her the value of life.

With each of these interim blessings, Megan has found hope, and her energies have been renewed. She has felt the love of her Heavenly Father. Because of her experiences, she is perhaps better prepared for life's challenges that await her. Perhaps these experiences have allowed her to look at the world differently or to provide understanding to others just like her. Regardless, she does, indeed, appreciate the blessings she has received and recognizes their origin. Her testimony has been strengthened as has her commitment to her husband.

Ardeth Greene Kapp

The biography of Sister Ardeth G. Kapp tells the story of a great woman's own struggle with infertility and her journey of faith. As a young woman, Sister Kapp, like most girls, pictured her future family as one with a husband and children. And, in time, she did marry; but when children did not bless her and her husband's lives in the time frame they anticipated, the couple became troubled with worry and concern. A multitude of tests and the expertise of doctors confirmed to Ardeth and her husband, Heber, that conceiving and bearing children would take a miracle.[5]

They had never contemplated the possibility that they would not have children. Like all who are infertile, Ardeth was not immune to the full range of emotions that accompanies this devastating and seemingly hopeless prognosis. As she walked through mists of darkness and "encircling gloom," she felt extreme sadness and agony and even wept at the thoughts that she might never hold her own children.[6] She relived the painful disappointments and doubts each month as she was reminded of her body's betrayal. Like most couples, she and her husband considered that perhaps they were being plagued with infertility because they were not righteous or worthy enough to have children.

Still, Ardeth and Heber believed in miracles, writes Anita Thompson, Sister Kapp's biographer. "They maintained a positive attitude regarding their eventual parenthood, fully believing that their desire for a large family would not be denied. They trusted that their Heavenly Father had heard their petition and would grant their deeply held longings for children."[7]

As Ardeth desired to know the will of the Lord and what purpose her life would fulfill, she continued to live a faithful life. She accepted callings and assignments with a willing heart; she found guidance and spiritual strength in fasting, prayer, the messages of priesthood blessings, attending the temple, scripture study, and being obedient to all of the commandments and promptings she received. She and Heber sought answers in the temple and felt the specific prompting that children would not be born to them in this life.[8]

Though painful, they could not deny that this was an answer from the Spirit; they accepted it and moved on, wondering why this blessing would be withheld from them. They considered adoption and went to the Lord in fasting and prayer about that path. However, they concluded that adoption was also not the answer.[9]

Because they had seen the power of obedience, they committed to following the direction they had received. Of course, this was not easy. As is common, Ardeth fought back feelings of envy as she observed the happiness that graced the lives of her friends as they began their families. In time, she learned to replace that envy with charity. When she felt helpless as those around her questioned why she and Heber remained childless, she sought peace through continued obedience. Although it was certainly difficult, she and Heber decided that they would rather celebrate family and children with those they love than choose to be withdrawn and isolated. They did not want their heartache to "prevent them from sharing in the happiness of others," Thompson writes.[10] Making this commitment allowed priceless relationships to be born, particularly with nieces and nephews.

As Ardeth began to accept childlessness, she searched to find meaning and purpose in her life—a life that was not going according to her plan. In her quest to live a life of meaning that would be acceptable to her Heavenly Father, she sought to make others happy.[11] She found answers in the words of her husband: "You need not possess children to love them; loving is not synonymous with possessing and possessing is not necessarily loving. The world is filled with people to be loved, guided, taught, lifted, and inspired."[12]

She served as a Young Women leader in various settings, as a member of Church curriculum committees, as a counselor and president in general Young Women presidencies, as a mission president's wife, and as matron of a temple. She has fulfilled many speaking requests, written numerous letters of encouragement, and spoken to couples desiring children. In each of these endeavors and beyond, she has made a lasting impression through "her warmth and her enthusiasm, her genuine concern for others, and her testimony."[13]

But, even as she filled her life with many great things, she had gentle, nudging reminders of the heartache and anguish in her soul. She says: "I keep thinking of my [patriarchal] blessing that tells me I'll know the Lord's will concerning me. I so want to fill the measure of my creation and do what it is I'm supposed to do. I've thought over the years that not having children would finally be a closed subject that was accepted and no more thought about—but I guess those feelings will always be there. More than anything else in the whole world, I'd like to have a family. . . . Sometimes I feel lonesome inside."[14]

Although she has not received the miracle of conception, Ardeth has experienced other significant miracles. She received the miracle of understanding Heavenly Father's will through specific revelation from the Spirit. It was because of this understanding that she was able to accept childlessness enough to live a quality life. She has been blessed with the vision to see and know what Heavenly Father needed her to do. And although her life unfolded differently than she anticipated, it was because of this vision that she found happiness. Additionally, as she reached beyond herself in love and provided strength to others, she was granted the miracle of joy. By receiving unexpected yet much needed love and strength from those she served, she was able to find fulfillment.

She also witnessed miracles wrought by the priesthood which she likens to a "reservoir of limitless power."[15] In profound blessings pronounced upon her, she felt her burdens literally being lifted from her shoulders.[16] Additionally, writes Thompson, she felt as though specific concerns she had were addressed, that the "blessing of children which they had desired had been withheld for a righteous purpose."[17] These blessings answered questions that had plagued her and provided peace to her aching heart.

In her journal she recalls: "If I had had this knowledge and feeling twenty years ago it would have been so much easier. I would have anguished less, but I would have been deprived of the spiritual growth which has come. This blessing was a confirmation to me that the Lord hears our prayers, and according to His wisdom and timing, tends to the welfare of His children."[18]

What life-altering miracles! Through her faith, Ardeth allowed for these miracles to enhance her life. Because she recognized these miracles, she saw evidence of Heavenly Father's hand in blessing her life. Despite receiving the miracle of being able to cope, the sting of infertility never went away from the life of this remarkable woman. In fact, Ardeth once said: "My desires for children of my own remains strong, and I think that's all right. Even though I accept the will of the Lord, I would not wish for us to ever lose our desire for a family."[19] It is refreshing to hear that there is nothing wrong with holding on to the desire to have a family.

Maren, Megan, and Ardeth Kapp—faithful, righteous, and deserving women. There are many others just like them. Each of them have experienced miracles, just as real and demonstrative of Heavenly Father's love as those who have received children after many years of waiting. Because of their unwavering faith, miracles and interim blessings became a part of their lives.

Elder Robert D. Hales taught us that "by design, most miracles are spiritual demonstrations of God's power—tender mercies gently bestowed through impressions, ideas, feelings of assurance, solutions to problems, strength to meet challenges, and comfort to bear disappointments and sorrow."[20] Because many miracles are quiet and gentle, they are easily overlooked. These humbling manifestations of His intimate and individual love for us must be identified and should not be discounted, for they are just as worthy of praise and gratitude! These miracles change lives in indescribable ways. They deserve sincere reverence and awe as do the hands from which they flow.

Recognizing daily miracles can help us see that our lives are of great worth to our Heavenly Father. We see that He is willing to make His hand apparent in our lives and to provide us with evidences that He is mindful of us individually. I know that as I see how He blesses me, I feel as if my life has meaning to Him. If my life has meaning to Him, why should it not have meaning to me?

So, let us ask again . . . do miracles always happen? Yes, miracles always happen. Look beyond the flashy parting of the Red Sea miracles, and acknowledge that miracles can be simple, private, and can occur daily for each of us. May your eyes be opened so that you may see miracles in your life.

Notes

1. Susan W. Tanner, "All Things Shall Work Together for Your Good," *Ensign*, May 2004, 105.
2. Dallin H. Oaks, "Miracles," *Ensign*, June 2001, 9.
3. Bible Dictionary, "Miracles," 732–33.
4. "More Holiness Give Me," *Hymns*, no. 131.
5. Anita Thompson, *Stand As a Witness: The Biography of Ardeth Greene Kapp* (Salt Lake City: Deseret Book, 2005), 128.
6. Kapp, *My Neighbor, My Sister, My Friend,* 126-127; Thompson, *Stand As a Witness*, 133.
7. Thompson, *Stand As a Witness*, 128.
8. Ibid., 129.
9. Ibid., 130.
10. Ibid., 128.
11. Ibid., 133.
12. Ardeth Kapp, "You're Like a Mother," *Ensign*, Oct. 1975, 58.
13. Thompson, *Stand As a Witness*, 250.
14. Ibid., 133.
15. Kapp, "You're Like a Mother," 58.
16. Thompson, *Stand As a Witness*, 229.
17. Ibid., 214.
18. Ibid.
19. Ibid., 135.
20. Robert D. Hales, "Personal Revelation: The Teachings and Examples of the Prophets," *Ensign*, Nov. 2007, 88.

CHAPTER FOUR

"If You Are Not a Mother, Then What Are You?"

have a vegetable garden. It is an untraditional vegetable garden that a green-thumb gardener would laugh at, but to me, it is a vegetable garden. My "garden" consists of a single tomato plant in a plastic pot on the small deck off of my kitchen. The wonderful thing about my garden is that it is thriving! My tomato plant has actually grown, is still green, and has beautiful yellow flowers on it giving me hope that it will produce delicious, red fruit.

This plant has taught me a little something about being fruitful, multiplying, and fulfilling the measure of its creation. We know that when planted under ideal conditions, a tomato plant will fulfill the measure of its creation by growing taller and stronger; it will be fruitful by developing tasty tomatoes; and it will multiply by producing additional plants. If conditions are less-than-ideal or untraditional, however, can this plant still be fruitful, multiply, or even fulfill the measure of *its* creation?

My little tomato plant is not growing under the most ideal conditions. Being in a pot all by itself, on a deck, and away from constant full sun can be considered untraditional. In fact, I did not even grow my plant from a seed since I knew my chances of being successful would be limited if I did not buy the plant already growing. Even under these conditions, however, my plant is flourishing. Because my plant is not dead, but rather is taller and will eventually accomplish something that it could not do three weeks ago, it is enlarging, magnifying, and improving itself. It is expanding itself, and it is prospering. It is fulfilling the very thing I wanted it to accomplish.

We all know that the natural course of human life is that men and women will get together and have children. Biologically, that is how our species is preserved; spiritually, that is how we accomplish Heavenly Father's plan of providing bodies for spirits, which plan ultimately leads to immortality and eternal life. Under ideal conditions, this process can be successful. Unfortunately, nature is often altered by less-than-ideal circumstances, some of which are beyond our control. Oftentimes, we can determine these circumstances and make changes that are necessary for success, but sometimes they are impossible to identify. For me, it might be that I am confined to a pot; for another person, it might be that they are not in full sun; for another it might be that they grow in solitude. The miraculous thing is that we can still become something greater than from what we were in the beginning and accomplish valuable things.

We often equate having children as being successful at being fruitful and multiplying; however, I believe there is a different way we can look at it. Let's go back to my tomato plant. Based on my garden limitations, I can only have one tomato plant. To me, my tomato plant is successfully fruitful as it grows and produces juicy fruit. I do everything in my power to make it successful by improving the conditions that I can control. I can water it. I can make sure that aphids and tomato worms stay away from it. And I can make sure it does not get dumped out of the pot. I am overjoyed by the progress that it makes each day as it gets taller, looks healthier, and gets closer to providing me with fruit. I hardly think about the fact that it will probably not produce additional plants for me to water and care for.

How can we expand our perspective to seeing that being fruitful and multiplying as being able to grow and extend ourselves and produce beautiful and delicious fruit rather than being paralyzed by the thought that we cannot have progeny?

Sister Ardeth G. Kapp wrote, "I will forever remember the day a child new to our neighborhood knocked on our door and asked if our children could come out to play. I explained to him, as to others young and old, for the thousandth time, that we didn't have any children. This little boy squinted his eyes in a quizzical look and asked the question I had not dared put into words, 'If you are not a mother, then what are you?' "[1]

When facing the challenge of infertility, it is common to feel displaced and to be left wondering who and what you are. You might think, "How can I be fruitful, multiply, and fulfill the measure of my creation if I cannot have children?" You may wonder what paths your life should take and if you will ever find joy equal to that found by a mother. At the same time, you may struggle to find some way to help others understand that a woman can fulfill *many* roles, not just that of a mother. Simply put, sometimes you may feel like you are drowning in adversity and see no way of measuring up to what you perceive as a "normal life."

During times when I have felt that I do not "measure up," I remember the story of Nephi's broken bow, found in 1 Nephi 16. This story has helped teach me how my own response to adversity is the first step in choosing the quality of my life.

As you recall, Lehi and his family were commanded to leave the comfort of their homeland to travel through a daunting wilderness to a promised land. On their journey, they were required to learn how to obtain food by hunting with bows and arrows. When Nephi broke his bow, and Laman and Lemuel's bows ceased to work properly, discouragement and uncertainty entered the picture. At this point, we see two responses to a threatening situation.

Not surprisingly, Laman and Lemuel *chose* to murmur and complain about their situation. Nephi, on the other hand, probably felt the same fear, exhaustion, and hunger as Laman and Lemuel, but his adversities made him proactive, and he decided to use his energy to produce a solution—he made a new bow and a slingshot.

When we experience significant setbacks in our wildernesses, we have a choice. We can follow the example of Laman and Lemuel by choosing to complain, murmur, and curse Heavenly Father for giving us a challenge. Or we can choose to identify how our lives will be changed because of the personalized challenge we face. Elder Richard G. Scott taught that we can ask questions such as, "Why does this have to happen to me? Why do I have to suffer this, now? What have I done to cause this?" but they do not serve a useful purpose. We can move ourselves in a positive direction, however, as we choose to follow Nephi's example and ask, "What am I to do? What am I to learn from this experience? What am I to change? Whom am I to help? How can I remember my many blessings in times of trial?"[2]

What attitude is more beneficial? The attitude of Laman and Lemuel or that of Nephi? Laman and Lemuel were occasionally motivated to be faithful so the Liahona would guide them to food. However, their resolve was far from sincere, and they never truly accepted any of the circumstances *or blessings* they received. Nephi, on the other hand, because of his willingness to rely on the mercies of the Lord, was given "understanding concerning the ways of the Lord" and knew that "by small means the Lord can bring about great things" (1 Nephi 16:29).

The way that we respond to our adversities is evidence of who we are and, ultimately, what we choose to become. If we respond like Nephi ,we will see adversity as an opportunity—a springboard to growing and learning. If we respond like Laman and Lemuel, we will curse God and choose a life of misery. We learn from these Book of Mormon friends that our ability to exercise faith determines our response. When we struggle with finding faith to believe in Heavenly Father's power, our spiritual vision is limited and all we can think to do is complain like Laman and Lemuel. When we are filled with faith, we respond like Nephi and choose to live life guided by the Spirit, trusting that Heavenly Father will "bring about great things." When in the darkness of a trial, it is often hard to be Nephi-like and it seems nearly impossible to muster the strength to not complain. But it is when we choose to be like Nephi that adversity refines us. Adversity does not diminish the quality of our lives; it does just the opposite . . . it enhances it.

Eliza R. Snow: A Latter-day Nephi

Eliza R. Snow was Nephi-like—she used her energy to form solutions and prevailed in the face of adversity. She chose to live a life guided by the Spirit and, with the help of Heavenly Father, the quality of her life was enhanced. Eliza can be remembered as a pioneer woman who left a legacy of music for us to enjoy today. Hymns such as "O My Father," "Truth Reflects Upon Our Senses," and "Behold the Great Redeemer Die" are among the songs she wrote to cheer the Saints, to teach principles of the gospel, and to express her personal testimony. Their messages transcend time and provide a spiritual education for us as we add them to our gospel understanding. Eliza was much more than a poetess, however. She was a woman of achievement and lived a remarkable life.[3]

Eliza was a woman of hope and optimism. She sought opportunity in every circumstance. She was a woman of intellect who was very skilled at organizing and leading. To Brigham Young, the prophet who directed the development of the Church in Salt Lake City, her intellect and opinion were highly valued.[4]

Because of his confidence in both her leadership and spiritual capacity, he asked her to direct the ordinance work performed by women in the Endowment House. While performing in this calling, Eliza saw the miracle of her health improve to the point that she could attend to her responsibilities. She was seen as a faithful woman with apparent gifts of the Spirit and was clothed with the sanctity found in the temple. While women looked to her for spiritual strength and direction, she nurtured them and became a companion as she loved and helped them.

Through her natural abilities to organize and lead with vision and wisdom, Eliza helped establish the Relief Societies in each individual ward after the exodus to Salt Lake; she helped develop the Young Ladies Retrenchment Association (now known as the Young Women organization) and the Primary Association. Additionally, she created the *Woman's Exponent*, a publication that addressed issues of interest to women. She encouraged women to receive training and education by organizing classes and directing women to go east to study medicine. She inspired many and provided hope through the gospel of Jesus Christ. Her life was centered on the women of the Church and the nurturing of others.[5]

But what does any of this have to do with infertility? Eliza was a woman who had every reason to be saddened by circumstance and by the unfairness of human life; yet, she did not allow despair to define her life. Authors Janet Peterson and Larene Gaunt wrote: "When Joseph and his brother Hyrum were martyred on June 27, 1844, Eliza was overcome with grief, unable to eat or to sleep, and even pled with the Lord to let her die also. One night as she lay in bed still sorrowing, Joseph appeared to her and told her she must not desire to die. Though his mission was complete, he said, hers was not—the Lord desired her to live and to help build up His kingdom. . . . "She put her grief to work for her and dedicated her talents to the Church."[6]

She received the miracle to move on and to find strength. She wrote, "I will smile at the rage of the tempest, and ride fearlessly and triumphantly across the boisterous ocean of circumstance . . . and 'the testimony of Jesus' will light up a lamp that will guide my vision."[7]

In the dark face of adversity, when she could have chosen Laman and Lemuel's path of despair, Eliza was able to find strength. It was her determination to be fearless, like Nephi, and to be guided by her testimony that allowed her to live a quality life and to "nobly [fulfill] the mission for which she was appointed."[8]

In the midst of grief, how did Eliza receive a vision to continue forward? Eliza was deeply committed to the gospel. Even though her parents fell away from the Church, she allowed her personal belief and conviction to be an anchor. She rejoiced in the gospel even during turmoil and tribulation.

She was also very faithful. She had a firm belief in the Savior and in the gospel. She was counted worthy enough to be entrusted with major Church responsibilities, to serve in the temple, and to be an instrument in Heavenly Father's hand to strengthen, serve, and to teach the women of the Church.

From Eliza, I have learned that a quality life is determined by what we are rather than by what we are not. We often spend so much time and energy dwelling on what we lack and how we do not measure up to others that we neglect areas of our lives that contain glimpses of greatness. By being trustworthy, people will look to us as examples of strength, and we will be entrusted with gifts to accomplish our individual missions. Are we allowing ourselves to become trapped for prolonged periods of time in our grief? Or are we being motivated by visions of our divine and individualized missions?

We must seek to know our individual missions, and then we must move forward with confidence, trusting that the Lord will guide us and help us to accept our lives as they are. We need to keep our spirits "strong and vibrant" as Eliza did. She did not allow her sorrow to overwhelm her life. She showed us that being active, reaching out to nurture others, and putting our talents to use will not only inspire others, it will inspire our lives as well. Her life was acceptable to her and to Heavenly Father because she chose to fulfill the unique mission He needed her to fulfill. Eliza was indeed fruitful, accomplishing great things in her life.

Finding Solutions the Brother-of-Jared Way

I love the manner by which the brother of Jared found solutions to his troubles. You may recall that he was given the task to transport his people from one land to another by crossing "the great waters" (Ether 2:22). The Lord guided his preparations, instructing him to build barges that would be "tight like unto a dish" that would not have windows (Ether 2:17). With great uncertainty of their destination, the people would be traveling in darkness, "encompassed about by the floods" (Ether 3:2). Additionally, they would not have control over where the barges went, nor would there be a means whereby they could receive fresh air. The brother of Jared had some very important tasks to fulfill to insure that his people would be able to survive the journey to a land "choice above all other lands" (Ether 2:7) safely. The brother of Jared "cried unto the Lord" (Ether 2:18) and received very specific directions as to what he needed to do in order to provide air.

However, when the brother of Jared prayed to receive instruction regarding having light in the barges, the Lord's response was much different. The Lord asked the brother of Jared a few questions: "What will ye that I should do that ye may have light in your vessels? For behold, ye cannot have windows, for they will be dashed in pieces; neither shall ye take fire with you. . . . Therefore what will ye that I should prepare for you that ye may have light when ye are swallowed up in the depths of the sea?" (Ether 2:23, 25). The Lord put the responsibility of finding a solution for light solely into the brother of Jared's hands.

As he dealt with his challenge, the brother of Jared could have allowed fear, inadequacy, and uncertainty to drive his response, but he did not. Instead, he exercised control and proactively sought a solution. He determined that he would have the Lord touch sixteen stones. These stones, once touched, would give light in darkness. He approached the Lord, saying, "I know, O Lord, that thou hast all power, and can do whatsoever thou wilt for the benefit of man; therefore touch these stones, O Lord, with thy finger, and prepare them that they may shine forth in darkness; . . . that we may have light while we shall cross the sea"

(Ether 3:4). As the finger of Christ touched those stones, the brother of Jared's solution to the problem of darkness was made acceptable to Christ, to Heavenly Father, and to him.

With light, the Jaredites began their journey. They "were tossed upon the waves of the sea before the wind" and "buried in the depths of the sea" (Ether 6:5-6), but they made it to the promised land. I love that it says that "the wind did never cease to blow towards the promised land" (Ether 6:8). The wind caused the tempests and buried them in the depths of the water, but it also propelled them in the direction the Lord intended for them to go.

Because of infertility, my life has often seemed dark, my path has seemed uncertain, and I have felt, at times, unable to steer my own course. Not long ago, I felt that I was not measuring up to what I wanted to be or what I thought I should become. It seemed as though my infertility was determining who I was, the path I was taking, and every other feeling I experienced. I felt out of control.

I needed to make decisions about my career, pursuing additional education, and a potential relocation for my husband's job. Ultimately, each of these decisions would be affected by what I would be doing six months from that time. Would I be pregnant? Would we be pursuing in vitro fertilization? Would we be taking a break from procedures? Uncertainty ruled my life, and I assumed the worst case scenario. I was convinced that things could not possibly get worse.

Additionally, I wondered what Heavenly Father wanted me to do. Did He want me to do all in my power to become a mother? Where was my life going? Am I pleasing Him by what I am doing now? These were all questions that played repetitiously in my mind and in my prayers. I was frustrated and lost. My answers came from this story of the brother of Jared.

Much like the brother of Jared, we need to listen to the specific directions Heavenly Father gives us. We then need to pursue a righteous path through prayerful consideration. Our path may seem untraditional, much like using small stones to light large barges, but that is all right. When we present our path to the Lord, we need to say, "I know that thou hast all power . . . therefore touch my life and prepare it that it may shine forth in darkness . . . that I may have light while I shall cross the sea." We can ask that He touch our lives, much like He touched those sixteen stones. The Lord can illuminate our lives, bringing light into what seems to be impenetrable darkness. When He touches our righteous lives, He makes them acceptable. He can make a life without children acceptable to Him, to Heavenly Father, and to us.

This light can then guide our lives, shining forth in the darkness of infertility, and can be filled with many meaningful things. Once our lives are made acceptable and are illuminated by Christ, the pains and difficulties may not cease. Instead, we will probably see that storms will continue throughout our lives. They will toss us about on the waves of the sea and bury us in the depths of the water. We can be assured, however, that in our faithfulness, the exalting power of our trials will propel us toward the promised land of eternal life.

Reclaim control of your life. Like Nephi, Eliza R. Snow, and the brother of Jared, you can choose a positive response to the setbacks in your wilderness. Try to keep the sorrows of infertility from burying you in the deep waters. Infertility does not have to halt or diminish your plans and potential. Instead, allow infertility to refine you and to carry you to the promised land of eternity. In the midst of it all, find happiness now rather than reserving it for later. Do what you love to do. Use your talents to improve the world around you—to replenish, to inspire, and to nourish. There are things you can do that no one else is capable of doing. Additionally, there are lives that only you can touch. Do not let infertility affect you so much that you stop living or allow your quality of life to become negatively altered. Elder M. Russell Ballard wisely said: "A quality life is one that positively influences others and makes the world around it a better place in which to live. A quality life is one that is constantly growing, expanding its horizons and enlarging its borders. A quality life is one that is filled with love and loyalty, patience and perseverance, kindness and compassion. A quality life is one that is based on eternal potential and not confined to this life only. A quality life is a life well-lived."[9]

A quality life produces delicious fruit. Notice that Elder Ballard did not say that being a mother was a requirement to living a quality life.

I am convinced that Heavenly Father is helping me become what He needs me to be. I am different today than I would have been if I had children earlier in my marriage. I have accomplished things I would never have been able to imagine were possible. I have different relationships with my family. My level of discipleship is different because of the callings I have had. I am in good health because I began running several years ago as a means to relieve stress and because my husband, Joel, and I took up cycling. My marriage is the best I could ever hope for because of what Joel and I have accomplished, experienced, and endured together. I am grateful for Heavenly Father's way of developing me into the woman He knows I can be. I believe that infertility can destroy or it can create.

Let our lives be illuminated—full of meaning and purpose. Let us recognize that even in less-than-ideal circumstances, we can find ways to enlarge, magnify, and improve ourselves. We can expand ourselves beyond what we were in the beginning and be fruitful, just like my tomato plant. We can prosper! We can fill the measure of our creation! If we are not mothers, what are we? We are women of faith who have great things to accomplish. Our lives can be "biographies of faith"; we can be women "whom God has honored because they relied on Him in times of their extremity."[10]

The next section provides ways to put your faith to work as you face your infertility. These strategies will help you move forward with the eyes of Nephi and with the trusting heart of the brother of Jared and, in the end, you will prove that "when he hath tried [you], [you] shall come forth as gold" (Job 23:10).

Notes

1. Kapp, *My Neighbor, My Sister, My Friend*, 123.
2. Richard G. Scott, "Trust in the Lord," *Ensign*, Nov. 1995, 17.
3. Janet Peterson and Larene Gaunt, *Elect Ladies* (Salt Lake City: Deseret Book, 1990), 30, 32, 36.
4. Peterson and Gaunt, *Elect Ladies*, 35.
5. Ibid., 36-37, 39-40.
6. Ibid., 30.
7. Ibid., 40.
8. Jacob Gates, as quoted in Peterson and Gaunt, *Elect Ladies*, 40.
9. M. Russell Ballard, *Our Search for Happiness: An Invitation to Understand The Church of Jesus Christ of Latter-day Saint* (Salt Lake City: Deseret Book, 1993), 74.
10. Howard W. Hunter, *That We Might Have Joy* (Salt Lake City: Deseret Book, 1994), 101.

Part Two

SINGING A NEW SONG: PRACTICAL STRATEGIES FOR COPING WITH INFERTILITY

CHAPTER FIVE

———— ∞ ————

Taking Action

L earning to cope, survive, and find peace with infertility is one of the
biggest challenges infertile couples face. The intensity of the disappointment that comes when you find out that you cannot "multiply and
replenish the earth" can be overwhelming. After all, it seems that the
measure of our creation is to bring children into this world, teach them
the gospel, and return to live eternally with Heavenly Father. That is the
great plan of happiness. Without fail, references are made to families,
parenthood, and children every Sunday at church. So how do you accept
that you may never experience what others are talking about—the very
thing you were supposed to be wired to do?

When Joel and I were first confronted with our infertility, I remember sitting numbly through Sunday School discussions about trials, where
general solutions for dealing with disappointments always included serving others, being more diligent about reading the scriptures, praying,
going to the temple, or simply having more faith. Whenever I heard
these responses, I would, with extreme spiritual immaturity, roll my
eyes. These answers seemed so empty to me because I felt that I had been
doing all of these things and they were not working—these simply stated
solutions were not solving my problem.

As human beings, we expect our actions to have a literal and direct
correlation to desired outcomes. When it is dark in the house, we
know that we can turn on the light (action) and it will no longer be
dark (desired outcome). It is not hard for us to believe that flipping a

light switch will provide light. But it is sometimes extremely difficult to see how being faithful and diligent will solve our problems; after all, we know that reading scriptures (an action) will not literally open fallopian tubes, alter hormone levels, or help with conception (a desired outcome).

In truth, however, the "Sunday School" answers really are right: we do need to increase our faith. But increasing our faith means more than feeling different inside or simply saying we have more faith today than we did yesterday. We consciously choose to have faith. Having more faith involves work and an active demonstration that we are truly trying. If we want a way to be provided, we must go and do *all* of the things we are asked to do. Even then, the outcome of our actions may end up being the ability to cope rather than the miracle we were hoping for. But, by working and demonstrating our willingness to do all those things God has asked us to do, *we enable* Him to bless us with both physical and spiritual things we need according to His plan. Remember, "I, the Lord, am bound when ye do what I say; but when ye do not what I say, ye have no promise" (D&C 82:10).

The chapters that follow are my list of "actions"—the things that have helped me cope with my infertility. The nature of coping strategies is not to solve the problem, but to give tools to survive. The strategies I have chosen to share include things you can do as you react to comments from others and give information about your challenges, as well as things you can do to strengthen and improve yourself emotionally, physically, spiritually, and socially. None of these ideas are particularly profound or earth shattering. In fact, some of them may seem cliché, but I hope you will read them anyway and perhaps try them. I hope that at least one will open your mind, eyes, and life to the possibility of healing and living in spite of your infertility.

CHAPTER SIX

———— ⌘ ————

Reacting to Comments from Others

One of the hardest things to deal with is leaving the house and facing people—including the things people say. We have all heard someone say, "Relax! You are trying too hard!" to a woman who wants to get pregnant. Maybe someone has even said it to you. This phrase can evoke feelings of frustration rather easily because it implies that a couple is doing something wrong. In actuality, some couples dealing with infertility truly need to "try harder" to conceive since the process is, in some way, flawed for them.

To those of you who have heard this phrase, I suggest that we use it as an evaluation tool. Consider the questions: Are you, as a couple, worrying so much about conception that the quest for it has become all consuming? Have you inadvertently allowed this one part of your lives and relationship to transform into an obsession?

Even though it is hard to admit, sometimes, the intense "trying" to conceive alters our lives in some ways: physically, as we are in constant stressful situations; emotionally, as we deal with inevitable setbacks; and socially, as we compare our "flawed" lives to those of our friends and family. Additionally, dealing with infertility can also alter marital relationships, as physical intimacy might become more of a chore, duty, or means to an end. Perfectly timed intimacy, exact temperatures, and other logistics become so much the focus that spontaneity, enjoyment, and marriage fulfillment are left behind. In the end, it is easy to allow intimacy to become robotic and obligatory. Simply, the "trying" becomes the priority. Perhaps that is what "trying too hard" means.

I am certain we could all sit down and make an exhaustive list of the hurtful things we have heard people say. Some I have forgotten, others make me smile, while others still haunt me. Here are a few I have collected:

"Just relax and stop worrying about it too much . . . then it will happen."

"It will all work out in the Lord's time."

"Don't worry. You will be blessed to be a mother in the eternities."

"So, when are you going to have a baby?"

"Enjoy your time together while you can."

"I bet working in the nursery is great birth control."

"You are still young, and there is plenty of time for children."

"Have you thought about adopting? You can always adopt."

"I know someone who adopted and got pregnant not long after."

"Why don't you just be happy with your life as it is?"

"You have no idea how lucky you are that you don't have to worry about children. You can have one of mine."

"Life doesn't begin until you have children."

Here are a few that I just could not believe:

"Do you not have children because you don't want them or because you can't have them?"

"Infertility might be a punishment for something you have done."

"Heavenly Father knows who should be a mother and who shouldn't."

"There aren't as many spirits needing to come to earth. Heavenly Father is running out because there is a limited supply."

"You haven't met your full potential until you become a mother."

How do you respond to comments like these? Some of them can arouse feelings of anger and cause a flood of uncontrollable sorrow. Others seem to chastise or imply that you do not measure up to what is expected or considered to be normal. Others make you feel that no one understands and that you do not fit in anywhere. Do you simply ignore the comments or questions? Or do you open the floodgates and tell everyone what is happening in your life? What do you do?

It has taken a long time to get to this point, but I am beginning to see comments and questions regarding my infertility as a door being opened for discussion. Infertility, however, is not an easy topic to discuss because of its sexual and intimate nature, the emotions involved, and sometimes the inability to find an appropriate time or the right words to use. When a discussion is opened by a comment from someone, remember that you do not have to offer some long, drawn-out explanation complete with talk of intercourse and fertilization. In fact, you don't even have to offer details. When you feel comfortable offering some information, it's best to keep it simple, direct, and maybe even a bit vague. Keep in mind that you do not have to share the entirety of your sorrow when people ask questions such as, "So when are you going to have children?"

Here are some suggestions of what to say when the questions come:

"We are ready for children whenever they join our family."
"There is a time and season for everything in life. Children come in a different time and season for every couple."
"Our family consists of me and my husband/wife right now."
"We are confronting some issues as we try to have a family. We are working with a highly skilled physician and feel confident in his/her abilities. We appreciate you being supportive and understanding."

I think I have used every one of these and several others; they usually move the conversation in another direction. Many times, responding this way makes the questioner realize the magnitude of the question they asked. So my suggestion to you is to come up with a response that you and your spouse will use when the situation arises. That way, you will be armed and prepared instead of being caught off guard. Coming up with responses to people's comments is a great activity for family home evening.

Remember to stay calm, cool, and collected. Be confident in your responses. Your responses should be positive and non-offensive—being rude or biting back is not a good path to take, even though it may seem like the best choice at the time. In the moment of being offended, I have wanted to bite back at unsuspecting questioners. To the question "When are your going to have children?" I have always wanted to use one of several responses: "Maybe nine months from last night," "We aren't a kid-friendly house—my white couch would be destroyed," or "I guess we just haven't figured out how to do it yet." Or to the question "Have you thought about adopting?" I would like to say, "No, have you?" Even though these comments may bring a momentary feeling of victory, what is it accomplishing?

I know that comments from others can hurt. I believe that, in the end, *most* people do not make comments or ask questions to be unkind or hurtful. Some people simply do not know what to say or how to say it in a way that demonstrates sensitivity. Some people believe that when they make comments they *are* being sensitive. They may have even thought about what they will say, perhaps thinking a touch of humor would help.

When dealing with less-than-ideal circumstances, sometimes we humans can be overly sensitive or emotional and perceive comments to have a different connotation than the speaker intended. I am the first to admit that, because we are human, it is easy to become offended, defensive, and to allow seemingly unkind comments to intensify within our hearts. Even though it is far easier to let those feelings fester, we must make the effort to let them go. Harbored anger and hurt can become destructive and has the capacity to lead to resentment, ill feelings, and the expression of additional unkind words (including words of criticism said to someone or behind someone's back), all of which can end with stressed or broken relationships. President Eyring taught "We must speak no ill of anyone. We must see the good in each other and speak well of each other whenever we can. . . . We must forgive and bear no malice toward those who offend us. The Savior set the example from the cross: 'Father, forgive them; for they know not what they do' (Luke 23:34)."[1]

I know I personally need to work on letting go of hurt feelings, not retaliating with unkind words, and learning to assume that people say things with the best of intentions. It is not always an easy task, but necessary, nonetheless. How we respond to the comments of others speaks volumes about us personally: we can either be seen as bitter, deeply angry, and unapproachable, or we can be seen as willing to educate others, open to sharing feelings as appropriate, and desirous to foster relationships of love and understanding. I believe that as our words are free from contempt and disrespect and are filled with meekness, love, humility, and understanding, we open our lives to much needed peace, an added portion of the Spirit, as well as opportunities to nurture loving relationships.

May I also recommend reading "Appendix A: Supporting Someone Who Has Fertility Challenges," which includes information that may be helpful to those who want to support a friend or family member dealing with infertility and would like to know how to better approach the topic and situation.

Note

1. Henry B. Eyring, "Be One," *Ensign*, Sept. 2008, 8.

CHAPTER SEVEN

---⚬⚬⚬---

How and When to Share Your Sorrow

How grateful I am that I live in today's world! Despite some of the destructive, frustrating, and sad things we see, we are quite blessed. In many ways, we are in a better place than we were generations ago. We have seen a social and relational evolution as each generation improves upon reactions to life's experiences, including how to communicate about difficult subjects. Once considered taboo, sharing feelings about intimacy and infertility has become more acceptable. While we are far from perfect, we must give ourselves credit for constantly fine-tuning our ability to be sensitive and respectful as we discuss something so sacred and private. As we have experienced this evolution, we have accomplished something extraordinary—we have paved the way for supportive relationships as well as the sharing of valuable knowledge.

I think back to my great-aunt and uncle. They were married in 1943 and established their life together in a small farming community in Tooele County, Utah. My great-uncle labored with his hands to add a chimney, windows, kitchen cabinets, and plumbing to the old family store, turning it into a warm, inviting home. Like most young couples, they had hopes of having children and raising them in this home and in this close-knit community. Children never came, however. Feelings of bitterness, sorrow, betrayal, and grief entered into their happy life, but they found a way to live beyond it. Nothing was really ever said about their childlessness. It was obvious that they were without child, but no one knew why, nor did they ask.

I do not know all of the circumstances, nor would I ever suggest that I could understand the situation as it was back then. But I can't help but wonder what my sweet aunt would say today. What would she say if she could share the feelings of her heart? Would sad feelings flow? Or would I hear a voice filled with confidence, knowing that her life was filled with specific, satisfying blessings and experiences tailored just for her? Oh, how I wish that I could sit down and talk to her face-to-face, candidly and without the socially imposed reservation of past generations. I know I would learn so much from her and I know that she would be blessed by sharing.

I believe that sharing the silent sorrow of infertility with family and friends, while difficult, can be therapeutic. Keeping sorrow completely silent really accomplishes only one thing: isolation.

At first, my husband and I thought that not telling our families every process and detail would protect us from having to share our disappointments with everyone. We also thought that it would protect us from what seemed like constant contrived questioning and people feeling sorry for us. In reality, we ended up denying ourselves loving support, faith-filled prayers, fasting, and the opportunity to demonstrate our confidence in our families.

Marriage and family therapist Ellen D. Speyer says that it is important to "include friendly, safe, supportive, and loving people in your world. You may not be ready to discuss this situation with everyone, but trusting a few friends or family members can help you to tolerate this period of stress and anxiety."[1] Part of coping with our uncertain world of infertility and overcoming the inevitable feelings of isolation is building trusting relationships with friends and family members.

There is power in sharing your sorrow. As you do so, however, be wise about who you tell, when you tell them, how you tell them, and why you tell them. My main concern with sharing was that the news would spread like wildfire, because I saw it happen with a dear friend.

Jessica and her husband were infertile. They had one daughter who came naturally after years of faith, tears, and many procedures;

and now they were experiencing the pain of infertility for a second time. After doses of fertility drugs, sperm testing, and much more, they decided that they would try IVF. After Jessica shared with several people in the ward that they were undergoing this intense process, it seemed to me that everyone knew almost instantly.

Jessica and her husband had been through the preparatory hormone injections and were at the point of retrieval and transfer. The Sunday the transfer was to take place, I heard a group of women talking at church about how Jessica's procedure was scheduled for that day, and that she would know if it was successful in two weeks. The ward's countdown had begun. At that moment, I made a conscious decision to not tell anyone in our ward about the processes we were going through—especially not in such detail that others would know the exact timing of my procedures. I was dumbfounded that Jessica's procedures had become the topic of casual conversation in a less-than-private place. If you are uncomfortable about this type of thing, it's wise to let those you tell know that you'd like them to keep quiet.

Who Should You Tell?

Who to tell is something you will want to think through very carefully. Do you want to share it with your immediate family? How about your extended family? Do you want to share it with those you serve with in the Primary or with your visiting/home teachers? How about your Relief Society president or your bishop? Do you want your co-workers or your boss to know? Some feel more comfortable keeping every detail between husband, wife, and Heavenly Father. Others tell only a few close family members and friends. The decision will be different for everyone.

Think about who you trust to be supportive, who you feel confident will support you through thick and thin. Consider who will keep information about your infertility confidential and will use the information you disclose wisely. Think about who will be the most sincere and who will respect your privacy. It may not be your closest friends. It may be someone you know who also experiences infertility. Choose people you will not regret telling.

Before you tell someone about your infertility, ask yourself, "Why am I telling this person?"

Reasons for telling people might include:

- You love them and know they will offer support.
- They have genuinely asked about your situation, and you feel confident in discussing the topic with them.
- You feel that your experiences will be beneficial to them.

Don't tell someone about your infertility just because they ask. Decide if they are truly concerned or if they are just trying to get the scoop. In a situation like this, you could always say, "Yes, we are experiencing some infertility problems and have decided to keep them to ourselves for now. I appreciate your concern."

Make sure that you establish your limits. Discuss with your spouse what you will share and with whom you will share it. Make sure these boundaries are clear between you and your spouse, and then maintain them. Remember that it is also a good idea to give your friends and family limits; they need to know what information needs to be kept quiet.

When Should You Tell?

The best time to tell others about your sorrow varies from couple to couple. You may choose to share when you find out the diagnosis, when a procedure fails, or when another starts. You may bring it up when someone you know confides in you that they are experiencing infertility. You may choose to tell about every detail or about selected procedures only.

For some, it helps to talk and share with others at the moment of disappointment—when the sadness and frustration are at their peak. For others, it is more comfortable to share when things are quiet—after decisions are made or when you are in better control of your emotions. Either way is fine. Some suggest that you designate a spokesperson. If family or friends want to know how you are doing, they can contact the designated spokesperson. You relay the information you do not mind others knowing to this spokesperson, who is then free to give the information out to those who ask. This method may work for you, or it may not. Keep in mind that sharing the happy news is easy, but sharing the disappointments can be nearly impossible.

My husband and I chose to tell our immediate families about our diagnosis after I had an exploratory laparoscopy in December 2003. We had been through three failed cycles of artificial insemination and had wondered for nearly a year what the problem might be. When the results of the laparoscopy included the fact that my fallopian tubes were severely damaged and that achieving pregnancy naturally would be nearly impossible, we decided to inform our immediate families. We made phone calls to each set of parents and to each of our siblings. We shared our quest over the past year, our disappointments, our lack of knowing where we would go from this point, our desire for keeping the news within the immediate family, and we requested some privacy. We were overwhelmed with their sympathy, their expressions of hope, and their promises that prayers would be said in our behalf. We left it at that.

When we decided to move forward with IVF in January 2005, we limited the people we told. We let our parents know. We kept it quiet because we felt that the disappointment that would come if it failed would be too overwhelming. When our cycle was cancelled because my ovaries were not responding to the medication, I was relieved that I would not have to go home and call ten or more people to let them know of the news. It was a quiet grieving.

With our second cycle of IVF in May 2005, we told the same people as before, with a few exceptions. As we experienced the disappointment of our remaining embryos dying, destroying our backup plan if the two we transferred did not implant, we felt our faith alone could not perform miracles. We told each of our siblings about our experiences. Each expressed feelings of love and a desire to pray in our behalf. Two weeks after our transfer date, our pregnancy test was positive, but not so positive. The doctors look for an hCG level of at least 100 to consider transfer a success and to move on to the next steps of IVF, which prepare the body to sustain a pregnancy. My hCG level was 12. I was told to return for a test in two days. If the second blood test resulted in a higher number there would be hope. If the level had decreased, we would need to live with a failed IVF cycle. We were not hopeful. We returned home, shed some tears, called our parents with the disappointing news and asked that they call everyone else. It was hard enough to tell my mother that the process had failed; there was no way that I would have been able to share that news with each of my siblings. My heart was broken.

Our families responded to our disappointment with expressions of love and respect. They admitted that there were no words that would make things better and simply said they were sorry. We appreciated their support and their apparent understanding of how they could not possibly comprehend the sorrow we felt.

During our experience of infertility, Joel and I have discussed with whom we wanted to share information and what exactly we would share. We had to reevaluate several times as circumstances changed, and we did not share everything. There are still things that remain between the two of us and will always be ours alone.

In the book *Infertility and Involuntary Childlessness*, Beth Cooper-Hilbert discussed the impact of having a social support system as we go through pivotal life events. She said, "Callan and Hennessey (1989) have found evidence of a connection between social support from friends and family and better recovery from stressful life events. Such reconnection involves conscious decisions about the extent of involvement with extended family—whom to tell and how much to tell—and how to establish new boundaries."[2]

Think about your social support system. Connecting with family and/or friends through the experience of infertility may be just what you need. You may want to have a conversation with significant people in your life and instruct them on how you would like be treated. Or you may simply want to keep quiet. No matter what you decide, it should be a joint decision between husband, wife, and Heavenly Father. Remember that we do not have to shut our feelings up inside and pretend that all is well. We can *share* and by doing so, we will strengthen ourselves and those who need it most.

Notes

1. Ellen D. Speyer, MFT, "Waiting, Wondering, and Worrying?" In*focus*, Summer 2005, 17.
2. Beth Cooper-Hilbert, *Infertility and Involuntary Childlessness* (New York: W. W. Norton, 56).

CHAPTER EIGHT

Physical Strategies

A nyone who reads a newspaper or magazine is constantly reminded that proper diet, appropriate exercise, and plenty of rest increase our daily capacities as well as our life span," says Patricia T. Holland.

> But all too many of us put off even these minimal efforts, thinking our family, our neighbors, and our other many responsibilities come first. Yet in doing so, we put at risk the thing these people need most from us: our healthiest, happiest, heartiest self. When they ask for bread, let us not be so weary and unhealthy that we give them a stone.
>
> The issue for me, then, is accepting that *we are worth the time and effort it takes to achieve the full measure of our creation*, and believing that it is not selfish, wrong, or evil. It is, in fact, essential to our spiritual development.[1]

What a perfect statement! Sister Holland reminds us that the plan is about each of us *individually*. We must "go and do" for ourselves in order to achieve our full measure of creation. And part of this is taking care of our physical selves. How do we do that? Let me suggest four ways.

Find Out the Cause of Your Infertility

I cannot stress this enough—not knowing why you cannot conceive causes deeper and darker feelings of sorrow. It adds an element of mystery and wonder to your pain. When you have a reason, or a prognosis, you can move forward and find solutions. You have somewhere to go. Dr. Russell A. Foulk, said, "Today, we have the ability to learn virtually every reason why a couple can not achieve a successful pregnancy" and "infertility is merely the result of a broken component or dysfunctional step within the reproductive system that keeps it from working. If we correct the broken step, then 100% of our patients can achieve a pregnancy."[2]

The sad fact is that "less than half [of couples having conception issues] seek help from a health care provider."[3] You may ask, why? For some it may be because of financial reasons, or because they may feel that if Heavenly Father wanted them to have children, He would provide a way. For another couple it may be because they feel that the intimate nature of infertility should be kept between a husband and wife. Others are reluctant because they are afraid that the answer will be that they will never have children. Others hold on to the hope that maybe next month will be the lucky one, while others are afraid of finding out what is required in order to make their dream a reality. Others wonder what the Church's stand is on infertility, the process of diagnosis, testing, and treatments. And others don't know who to go to and where to start their quest.

A friend of mine had been married for over five and a half years before their infertility was diagnosed. She and her husband waited until after they were both out of school, and he had secured a job with good insurance before they started their quest. Once they were assured that their insurance would help with the expenses, they sought help from an OB/GYN. After a series of tests, OB/GYN #1 could not determine a cause. Nor could OB/GYN #2. My friend and her husband were understandably frustrated and were not quite sure what to do. It was at this point that she and I spoke. I directed her to a list of specialists where she found one that would be covered on her insurance. The specialist found a cause! He told my friend that her condition was rare and that in the many years he had been practicing, he had only seen a handful of women with the same problem. The encouraging part was that the condition could be fixed with a simple surgical procedure. What an answer to prayers! And what great relief! After an extensive quest and a mixture of emotions, my friend had a diagnosis and a prognosis. The surgery was performed, she recovered, and eight months later, she was pregnant.

A health care provider can help you find out a "why" which often leads to a "how." As the old adage says, "Knowing is half the battle." Knowing what is happening with your body or your spouse's body is an important step on the path to coping and understanding.

I think I knew all along. At the age of fourteen, I suffered a severe infection resulting from a ruptured appendix that caused significant damage to my fallopian tubes. At that point in my life, I knew in my heart that I would not bear children. At fourteen, the day I would be a mother seemed so far off; I simply didn't fully understood the prognosis or have the ability to predict the extent of the long struggle ahead of me.

Even though I knew there would be some sort of struggle ahead, I did not want to admit it. I wanted to leave room for divine intervention—a miracle of sorts. After being married for several years and not becoming pregnant, reality set in. Even though I knew why, I wanted confirmation—medical confirmation. That is when my husband and I started our quest. I was not surprised that artificial insemination did not work once, twice, or even three times. I also was not surprised when, during a laparoscopy, my OB/GYN found both of my fallopian tubes to be "hydrosalpinges, with the fimbriated ends obliterated and densely scarred," according to my medical file; they were unable to function normally. At that point, what I always knew had been confirmed. I had answers. I knew that conceiving would be a great challenge, if not an impossibility. Now I could pick up and move on. Moving on meant taking a turn on a path that I did not expect and researching other means of reaching the worthy goal of motherhood.

Find the Right Doctor

My husband and I had just moved to a new city, so I asked around to find the best OB/GYN possible. Once I had found one, I sat in his office, handed over my carefully organized medical file, and explained to him that I was not just any ordinary new patient: I knew that I was experiencing infertility. I summarized what he would read in the pages of my medical file and told him that I wanted to move forward to find out what I could do to conceive. After he reviewed the file and asked me some questions, he gave me a list of options. He told me he could do some preliminary diagnostic tests, he recommended an exploratory laparoscopy to be done by a doctor in his practice, and he wanted to refer me to a reproductive endocrinologist. He told me the name of a specific reproductive endocrinologist and assured me that he would be a perfect fit with my personality.

My OB/GYN was right. The reproductive endocrinologist *was* the perfect doctor for my husband and me. Not only was he one of the biggest names in reproductive medicine in our area, he made us comfortable, he shared our values, and we felt that he was committed to helping us conceive.

I was lucky. Finding the right doctor is no small task. It is more involved than simply looking up "Conception Doctor" in the phone book. Since this particular doctor will probably see more of you than you want and will be involved in the most intimate part of your life, it is important that you feel comfortable with him or her and confident that he or she has your best interest in mind.

Unfortunately, not everyone has a positive experience with finding the right doctor. My friend Debbie's quest for finding the right doctor has been a difficult journey. Debbie's first OB/GYN (Doctor #1) was curious about possible endometriosis and referred her to a specialist. She called the specialist (Doctor #2) and only ever saw the nurse practitioner in the office. When Debbie indicated that she was interested in having an exploratory laparoscopy to determine endometriosis, the nurse practitioner told her that they had to do other tests prior to committing to the surgical procedure.

Between Debbie's timing and the doctor's timing, the tests were never performed nor was the surgical procedure. Debbie became frustrated that the process was so complicated, that she never actually saw the doctor she was referred to, and felt that there wasn't anyone particularly committed to listening to her or helping her. In her frustration, she went to another physician. Doctor #3 did a hysterosalpingogram (HSG), and felt there was no need for a laparoscopy, and jumped straight into artificial insemination. Failures began to pile up as did the dollar signs and the frustrations. At this point, Debbie and her husband moved and needed to find a new doctor. She was sure that this would prove to be a fresh start and that she could finally find a doctor that could help them.

Debbie found a great choice for an OB/GYN (Doctor #4)—he was an OB/GYN who specialized in infertility. She was sure that this would be perfect since she would not have to jump between doctors for regular gynecological issues and for infertility, and this doctor could provide consistent care. Over time, Doctor #4 seemed wishy-washy. Debbie felt like he often forgot that she was even pursuing a diagnosis of infertility, he left a lot of decisions up to her, he did not take time to explain procedures, and generally seemed scattered. While under his care, Debbie began two regimens of Clomid, but neither proved successful. As Debbie continued to have symptoms that seemed to her like endometriosis, she took her concerns to Doctor #4. To Debbie, the doctor seemed to discount her concerns and was certain that her own diagnosis of the problem was incorrect. Additionally, billing became a nightmare because it seemed that infertility procedures were getting crossed with regular gynecological services.

Debbie felt like she had been going to the wrong doctors for too many years and wanted to find someone different. She spoke to various friends about their experience with their fertility doctors and eventually found Doctor #5. She was excited that his Saturday appointments were not charged at a higher rate and that his new patient questionnaire asked her what she thought about her infertility. Immediately, she felt that this doctor was sensitive to the unpredictable schedules as well as the financial strain and the emotional issues that couples face through the process of fertility treatments.

After looking through her new patient questionnaire and asking Debbie a few questions, Doctor #5 simply looked at her and said "You know what is wrong, don't you?" When she affirmed that she truly felt that her problem was endometriosis, he validated her concern and said, "You are probably right." Doctor #5 instantly made her feel empowered and as though she might know her body better than anyone else. He questioned why a laparoscopy had not already been done, why a doctor jumped straight into artificial insemination, and why a doctor tried artificial insemination without prescribing Clomid. Debbie's confidence was being strengthened by the minute! When this doctor gave two options, with one being a laparoscopy, Debbie knew immediately that it was the option to take. Finally, after so many years, she would no longer have to wonder if her infertility was being caused by endometriosis—she would know for certain. Her appointment for the laparoscopy was scheduled less than two weeks after her initial consultation with Doctor #5.

When I spoke with Debbie the day before her surgery, she was nervous about the unknown but she was even more eager to find out what the doctors would see. We talked about how, if she did indeed have endometriosis, it would prove difficult to not place blame or to regret the process of the past five years. We both agreed, however, that perhaps the most beneficial thing she could do was to focus her energies on the future. She was confident that regardless of the result, questions would be answered, mysteries unfolded, and a prognosis determined. This was a day she had looked forward to for a long time.

The result: stage three endometriosis with severe damage done to her fallopian tubes, which could not be corrected. Not only was the diagnosis disappointing, the prognosis was even more grim since IVF would probably be their only option. Yet, Debbie was content that something had been discovered. With the news, Debbie's emotions and feelings were so varied and confused. While she felt encouraged by answered questions, new questions were presenting themselves. How long had the endometriosis been growing? Why did it have to be so bad? Now that most of it had been removed, would it intensify as it grew back? Would her tubes ever function normally? Would the pain of her menstrual periods be just as bad as before? Would IVF even work? Reflecting on the experience, she remains grateful that she finally found a doctor who listened to her, and even more, that she had the courage to continue her quest to find the right doctor for her needs.

Could Debbie's infertility have been diagnosed sooner if she had found Doctor #5 before Doctors #1–4? Perhaps. What I think we learn from Debbie's experience is that the doctor can make all the difference. Before she met Doctor #5, she was discouraged by her situation. Not only was she frustrated with her doctors, she felt like her options were limited, she did not feel that her concerns were being considered, and the clock was ticking. When she met Doctor #5, her attitude about infertility changed. She was filled with greater hope, she was happier, and she was excited with the possibilities ahead. That is why you need to find the right doctor!

Before you choose a physician, sit down as a couple and think about what you are looking for. Do you want a male or female doctor? How close do you want the doctor to be to your home? Would it be better for him to be located closer to work? What credentials do you expect her to have? How will you know if the doctor shares your same values? What kind of an atmosphere do you want the doctor's office to have? Do you want a doctor who has the wisdom of practicing for many years or one who is new in the industry? What kind of flexibility do you want with your schedule? Remember that your most fertile times do not always fall during weekdays. What do you want to see in the doctor's staff? How do you expect to be treated on the phone or when you go into the office? Are there any doctors covered on your insurance? Oftentimes you are limited by insurance or cost of services. These are very important parts to the equation and should certainly be considered.

Once you have a "sketch" of what you expect, you can start with your OB/GYN. Sometimes you will find an OB/GYN who specializes in infertility and can do testing, prescribe medications, and can perform some procedures. With these specialized OB/GYNs, you can sometimes solve your fertility problem or at least have some questions answered before escalating it to a reproductive endocrinologist.

If you exhaust your options with your OB/GYN, use him as a resource instead. Most likely, he has a network of reproductive endocrinologists to which he can refer you. Additionally, do not be afraid to ask around; ask friends who are experiencing infertility about their doctors. There is nothing wrong about asking them what they like about their doctor and what they do not like. Their experience can provide you with the needed information as you look for a doctor to help you. Do not be afraid to visit various doctors' offices. I am convinced that you can *feel* if a place will be the right fit. If you feel uncomfortable, be sensitive to that feeling.

If you choose a doctor and begin to feel like she might not be exactly what you need or that you feel uncomfortable, there is nothing wrong with going somewhere else. You may feel that your opinion is not valued, that your doctor continues to try the same procedure over and over again, or that your doctor acts annoyed with your questions. Do not feel obligated to stick around. You do not want to waste precious time.

Your doctor plays a vital role in how you feel about your infertility. When you find the right doctor, you will feel confident and hopeful. You will feel energized. You might even feel that you have options. Each of these things will help heal some of the feelings of frustration and sorrow.

Take Care of Yourself

Doctors have found that what we eat, how much we weigh, the frequency and type of exercising we do, and other lifestyle habits affect our ability to conceive.[4]

Make sure you sleep enough, find an exercise plan that works for you, and commit to eating well. There is great power in health. Two of my favorite scriptures talk about the blessings received from healthy living. The first is found in Doctrine and Covenants 88:124: "Cease to be idle; . . . cease to sleep longer than is needful; retire to thy bed early, that ye may not be weary; arise early, that your bodies and your minds may be invigorated." The second is found in Doctrine and Covenants 89—the Word of Wisdom. The promise to those who live according to this health code involves "health in their navel and marrow to their bones; And [they] shall find wisdom and great treasures of knowledge, even hidden treasures; And shall run and not be weary, and shall walk and not faint" (vv. 18–20).

I know from experience that as you deal with the challenges of infertility that you need as much help as you can get. You need your mind to be invigorated so that you can weigh all aspects of a decision. You need your body to be invigorated (not weary or faint) so you can handle medical treatments. You need "wisdom and great treasure(s) of knowledge" as you study procedures and their ultimate implications.

Perhaps you have felt the power of physical health. I know I have. On the days that I drink enough water, eat right (meaning that I eat things that are colorful and fresh rather than brown and sweet), exercise, and do not "sleep longer than is needful," I have a natural high. I have energy. I feel more capable of accomplishing the things on my list. I also feel that my mind is clear, and I think more positively. When I feel more upbeat, I honestly think that the Spirit is with me more abundantly on these days as well. There is great wisdom and power in sleeping well, eating right, and exercising.

When we were in the midst of one of our IVF cycles, I found exercise to be therapeutic. The daily injections in my hips were not only causing a great deal of pain and bruising, but they were causing intense swelling as well. Perhaps you can imagine my discouragement because I had to go to extraordinary means to do something I thought should be basic—conceiving—and now, my pants wouldn't fit! Sleeping was painful because I could not put pressure on my hips without horrible pain, sitting for long periods of time was uncomfortable, and walking was miserable. You may be asking, "So, how exactly was exercising therapeutic?"

My sister and I had the goal of walking together every day. During this cycle of IVF, we continued to follow our daily walk routine. It proved to be a lifesaver! Some days were particularly difficult, and I wanted to shut myself up emotionally and physically, but my sister knew I needed to get out and walk so she would encourage me, strongly. The therapeutic part was getting out into the sunlight, breathing fresh air, seeing the beauty of the world, talking to my sister, and being as active as I could be. I cannot remember everything we talked about, but I know that the physical activity somehow increased my emotional capacity as I dealt with the frustrations of the time.

Fertility treatments not only cause stress, but they alter a woman's body in many ways. You may have heard of some of the biggest complaints: gaining weight, feeling like you are going through menopause, thinking you are a teenager again because somehow your acne has come back, fluctuating emotions, bloating, headaches, nausea, fatigue, insomnia, depression, and anxiety, to name only a few. As your body goes through this mixed bag of side effects, often the last things you will want to do is exercise or eat well. But mustering the strength and stamina to do even the simplest exercise and improving your diet by adding another glass of water or eliminating just one unhealthy thing will lead you in the right direction.

Try to Stay Normal . . . Make Plans . . . Live

What would you like to accomplish in your life? I am sure that you have other life goals that do not involve children. Do not let infertility get in your way. To a woman discouraged because she was not married and had not begun a family, Sister Ardeth Kapp said, "Plan your life as if you were never going to get married. Do things that will fulfill you. If you do get married, great! If you don't, you will still have a full life."[5]

May I add: "Plan your life as if you were never going to have children. Do things that will fulfill you. If you do end up having children, great! If you don't, you will still have a full life." There are other things that can bring great meaning into your days. Decide what you are going to accomplish and do it! President Spencer W. Kimball said, "We realize, of course, there are some women who cannot have children, some men who cannot reproduce. The Lord will take care of all that if we have done everything in our power, if we have done what we could to make ourselves normal and productive and to follow the commandments of the Lord."[6]

Are you being productive? Your ability to be productive does not have to be affected by your ability to be reproductive. Do not put your life on hold while you tread through infertility. Expand your vision of yourself and find room to be more than infertile. Go on trips, learn to paint, develop one of those talents that might be hiding under the bushel. Dr. Beth Cooper-Hilbert says that other life pursuits "are adaptive ways to cope with . . . emptiness. . . . [They are] ways to regain perspective and to replenish."[7]

If you put your life on hold, you will miss wonderful experiences. Besides, continuing to live will grant you the ability to cope with your sadness by providing wonderful outlets for emotion.

Notes

1. Jeffrey R. Holland and Patricia T. Holland, *On Earth As It Is in Heaven* (Salt Lake City: Deseret Book, 1989), 66; emphasis added.
2. Russell A. Foulk, MD, "Common Obstacles to IVF Success," In*focus*, Fall 2003, 11.
3. Beth Cooper-Hilbert, Infertility and Involuntary Childlessness, 9.
4. See Michael Steinkampf and Karen Hammond, "Lifestyles of the Fit and Fertile," In*focus*, Winter 2004, 7.
5. Anita Thompson, *Stand As a Witness*, 314.
6. Spencer W. Kimball, *Teachings of Spencer W. Kimball*, ed. Edward L. Kimball (Salt Lake City: Bookcraft, 1982), 330.
7. Cooper-Hilbert, *Infertility and Involuntary Childlessness*, 74.

CHAPTER NINE

Emotional Strategies

Once you begin taking care of your physical self, you may automatically notice a boost in your emotional state. The two typically go hand in hand, after all. Eating right, exercising, and getting enough sleep relieves stress and increases the energy you need to keep a positive outlook on life. In many difficult situations, however, you can't simply exercise, eat right, or sleep enough to maintain a healthy emotional state; you need to work at that too. Here are several "emotional solutions" for couples dealing with infertility.

Know That You Are Not Alone

There is great power in knowing that others have the same problem as you do; it pulls you away from feeling alone and isolated.

I remember the first visit with our reproductive endocrinologist. I remember thinking that we were at our last resort, that our options would be limited, and that whatever he suggested would cost a lot of money. I also remember hoping that perhaps he could solve my problem and grant me the thing I wanted most. We handed him my carefully collected, organized, and very thorough medical file. He briefly flipped through the thick stack of pages, asked a few questions, and then told me that I was not alone. He explained that he has seen many women whose infertility is the result of a ruptured appendix; in fact, he made it sound like it was not uncommon for incidents of ruptured appendices to result in infertility. I was shocked. Up until that very moment, I was certain that I was the only unlucky one. In that one statement—said quite matter-of-factly, I might add—he offered me a glimmer of hope. Suddenly, I didn't feel so alone.

As mentioned previously, statistics show that one in seven couples have difficulty conceiving. That means in an average-sized ward, there could be more than a handful of couples who know how you feel. Do you know who they are? Do they know who you are? You do not have to feel so alone.

There is also great power in knowing that others know how you feel. I have sat in Relief Society countless times, looking around at the sisters and being certain that none of them knew how I felt. I was sure that they had no clue what it was like to feel such deep sorrow and grief. Over time, I have learned that I was wrong. Perhaps every woman does not know what it is like to be infertile, but without question, every single one of those sisters know with firm reality what it feels like to be cheated or defeated by mortality. Our circumstances are different, our trials diverse, but we have all wept because of heartache, misery, disappointment, and guilt when life does not turn out the way we desired or felt that it should. How common we really are!

Has this discovery lifted my burden entirely? Perhaps not. Do I think that a sister who has experienced sorrows such as the bitterness of divorce, the betrayal of being thirty-five and single, or the challenges of being a single mother will know how to nurture my tender and aching heart? Yes, I believe she can. Because she has known the bitter, *if* I allow her to, she can run to my aid and can help my wounded heart to heal. Our individual sufferings refine us, help us to become instruments, and assist us in keeping the command to "succor the weak, lift up the hands which hang down, and strengthen the feeble knees" (D&C 81:5).

Sure, you can discount a sister's desire to reach out to you. You can think that she could not possibly know what you are experiencing. You can choose to live alone in your misery. Or you can live side by side and begin to communicate heart to heart. We all have reason to be disappointed by life. Find comfort in knowing that others can understand, strengthen, and lift you, even if they know nothing of the sadness of infertility. As you recognize how similar you are to others, you choose to be understood. You choose to not be alone.

Realize That Infertility Is Not Your Fault

Infertility is not your fault—and it certainly does not make you any less of a person. Very few cases of infertility result from conscious choice. Even though you may feel that you are the reason for your infertility, find a way to convince yourself that it is your mortal body that is not cooperating with your desire to have children. Do not allow Satan to talk you into thinking that you caused your infertility or that it is because you did something wrong. That is one of his deceptive fabrications. Remember, he is eternally miserable, and he will do anything in his power to help you be miserable just like him (see 2 Nephi 2:27).

Even though conceiving and giving birth are specific traits and abilities husbands and wives have been divinely given, the fact that you cannot have children does not mean you are less of a person. Men, you are still men. Women, you are still women. Your body is still a temple that houses your spirit. Your spirit may become frustrated because of the limitations of the physical body, but in order to fulfill your divine potential, your spirit must accept what it has to work with and move forward. Remember, your identities should be defined by who you are and not by what you cannot do.

Mourn

With infertility, explains psychologist Dr. Beth Cooper-Hilbert, "there are multiple losses: loss of children, genetic continuity, pregnancy, control, and loss of an important life goal."[1]

And every month when menstruation begins, these losses are relived. Disappointment is inevitable. Mourning is an essential and healthy part of dealing with disappointment. Dr. Cooper-Hilbert says, "Spouses go through stages of mourning much like they would with terminal illness or the death of a loved one. They experience a deep sense of loss each month with the onset of menstruation."[2]

Give yourself permission to experience the full range of emotions. It is okay to cry. It is okay to feel sad. It is okay to be angry. Recognize that your feelings are normal. Allow yourself time away from regular life. Give yourself permission to mourn. Mourning can cleanse your soul of sadness.

On two separate occasions, Jesus experienced the loss of a dear friend, and through these experiences we can be taught about mourning. Shortly after John the Baptist's tragic death, the disciples informed Jesus of what had occurred. I am sure Christ was deeply troubled. John had not only baptized Him but was also a relative and a trusted friend. Upon hearing the news, Christ suggested that they depart into a "[solitary] place, and rest a while" (JST, Mark 6:31). In a time of great emotional unrest, Christ wanted to be alone, away from the multitudes. Of course, He had crowds of followers pressing in on Him, and He took compassion on them before departing immediately, but He did eventually separate Himself from the responsibilities He was engaged in and from those He was with so that He could mourn (see Matthew 14:13).

Lazarus was another friend of Jesus; in fact, the scriptures say that Jesus loved Lazarus and his sisters, Mary and Martha. Shortly after Lazarus died, the Savior went in to see Lazarus's body, and upon seeing his friend, lifeless before Him, "Jesus wept" (John 11:35). Christ had experienced a loss—a friend had died and He was overcome with emotion.

In our times of sorrow, we too can mourn. May I suggest that we follow the example of Christ and depart for a time from the cares of the world to a place of meditation and solitude? That time in a solitary place can be used for shedding tears and pleading with Heavenly Father.

When we learned that our second IVF cycle was not productive, Joel and I cried together. We spent the rest of the day alone. We ate out for lunch *and* for dinner. We laid low and watched a movie that night. We discussed our sorrows. We wondered why Heavenly Father had allowed us to spend thousands of dollars on something that would not work. We agreed that we did not understand His particular plan for us, but that there must be some sort of a plan. We allowed ourselves to mourn that day. Were we back to normal the next day or the next? No. The sting of sorrow was still there, but we did not feel like crying every two seconds. Why? I think three things contributed to our ability to handle the situation.

One, I truly believe that we gathered strength from prayer. When we arrived home after receiving the news, we prayed for comfort, peace, and a greater understanding—quite honestly, that was a very hard prayer to offer. Two, I think that sharing a day of mourning allowed us to release a good portion of our emotions. Three, the wonderful support of family helped us greatly. My compassionate sister invited us over to dinner the following day. She did not force us to join them. And our loss was not the topic of dinner conversation. Allowing time for our hearts to heal enough to continue on was pivotal in our ability to cope with these feelings of great sorrow.

Consider Seeking Help

Each day of infertility is different, and emotions change constantly. Allow yourself to feel them. As you do so, it can be difficult to know when your emotions have gone too far and have entered a realm where you need professional help.

Linda Hammer Burns, in her article titled "When to Seek Professional Help," suggests that you seek help from a counselor or therapist when:

- You have felt sad, depressed, or hopeless for longer than two weeks.
- You have noticed changes in your appetite, either eating more or less than usual.
- You are having trouble sleeping or are sleeping more than usual. You awaken not feeling rested.
- You feel anxious, agitated, and worried much of the time.
- You have panic attacks—particularly related to infertility situations or issues.
- You feel lethargic or have lost interest in usually enjoyable activities.
- You have trouble concentrating, are easily distracted, and/or have difficulty making decisions.
- You have persistent feelings of worthlessness or guilt.
- You feel easily irritated, angry, and frustrated.
- You have thoughts of death or dying.
- You have lost interest in intimacy.[3]

As members of the Church, we are fortunate to have LDS Family Services, which provides affordable counseling by licensed counselors. These counselors share LDS values and core beliefs. They can be helpful as you try to fit infertility into an LDS perspective.

Notes

1. Cooper-Hilbert, *Infertility and Involuntary Childlessness*, 34.
2. Ibid., 39.
3. Linda Hammer Burns, PhD, "When to Seek Professional Help," http://www.resolve.org/site/PageServer?pagename=cop_mis_sph.

CHAPTER TEN

------ ⪦⪧ ------

Spiritual Strategies

I n Part One we discussed spiritual healing by focusing on stories from the scriptures and modern-day Latter-day Saint women who have dealt with infertility. Many of the things these women have done to improve the quality of their lives are things you can do also. I've included in this chapter those "spiritual strategies" that have become most powerful in my own life. These strategies are most effective when we accept Christ's invitation to become more like Him. Our actions must be more than simple, outward performances of keeping commandments and covenants. Rather, our hearts and minds must truly become like His, such that we naturally do the things that will help us grow spiritually. This is a perfect opportunity to spoil yourself spiritually! May we adopt Moses's profound words to the Children of Israel, "take heed to thyself, and keep thy soul diligently" (Deuteronomy 4:9). As you read this section, consider which of these strategies might be most helpful as you diligently seek to deepen your discipleship, to rely more on the merits of our Savior, and to strengthen your faith in a very perilous time.

Pray

"Pray always, that you may come off conqueror" (D&C 10:5). Pray for understanding. Pray for guidance. Pray for doors to be opened—and for the patience to wait for them to open. Pray for peace. Pray that others might understand, and that you may be blessed with a greater perspective. Pray that you will not drown in your sorrow. Pray that you will have the ability to discover who you truly are aside from your infertility, and pray that you will grow in your understanding and testimony of Jesus Christ. Remember that all of the infertile couples from the scriptures had a relationship with the Lord. You too must pray so that your relationship with Heavenly Father and Jesus Christ will grow. How can you expect a miracle from your Father in Heaven if you hardly know Him?

Prayer is a vehicle—it is the way by which we speak to our Heavenly Father. We are fortunate to choose the quality of our prayers; we can merely say the same prayer night after night, or we can choose to truly communicate with our Heavenly Father. To communicate means to have an interchange in which we become connected to someone else. It means that we clearly reveal our thoughts so that we may be understood.[1]

Do you "clearly reveal" how you are feeling to your Heavenly Father? Does He know from your mouth what you are experiencing? He knows these things by the simple fact that He is omniscient (all-knowing), but has He heard it from you? It is when we *choose* to share with our Heavenly Father that we invite Him to be a part of our lives, to be a part of the decision-making process, and to help us through every moment of our lives. Allowing Him to "talk back" through the whisperings of the Spirit, through the words in the scriptures, or through someone else completes the interchange.

Our connection with Heavenly Father can improve as we pray vocally. President Spencer W. Kimball admonished us that we "ought to find, where possible, a room, a corner, a closet, a place where we can 'retire' to 'pray vocally' in secret. We recall the many times the Lord instructs us to pray vocally: 'And again, I command thee that thou shalt pray vocally as well as in thy heart; yea, before the world as well as in secret, in public as well as in private.' (D&C 19:28.) So central is this to our prayers and personal religious life."[2]

It seems that when I pray by simply thinking words in my head, my prayers tend to be repetitive, I get lost in what I am saying, and sadly, I sometimes fall asleep. I have noticed a dramatic change in the quality of my prayers when I petition Heavenly Father by saying each word aloud. The words I say, the things I express gratitude for, my requests of my Heavenly Father, and the tone of my words become more meaningful and deliberate. When I pray vocally, I think more about the content of my prayers, and they become a spiritual communion with Heavenly Father.

The Atonement was the most excruciating and painful experience any one person has ever endured. Because He suffered the pains of all the earth, Christ suffered in agony. In Luke, we read, "And being in an agony he prayed more earnestly" (Luke 22:44). Next to this passage in my scriptures, I have written, "How often when we are in an agony, do we pray *more* earnestly?" I would venture to say that when we experience agonies in our lives, we are likely to pray less earnestly or to not pray at all. Why? Sometimes, prayer seems to be the last thing we want to do. When we feel agony or when things do not go the way we plan, we feel betrayed by the One who loves us most. We allow ourselves to become bitter.

This is how I felt when we came home after being told our second IVF attempt was unsuccessful. Unfortunately, I did not have very many good things to say to my Heavenly Father. I felt that I had done everything in my physical, emotional, spiritual, and financial power that I could, and I was expecting the grace of the Savior to make up the difference. So, Joel prayed. He prayed that we might experience a greater understanding of Heavenly Father's plan for us and how this new disappointment fit into that plan. He prayed that we might be comforted and find peace. By that evening, I prayed with great intensity, expressing my feelings to Heavenly Father. He also expressed His feelings of comfort to me. When you *kneel*, verbalize, and pray more earnestly, the bitterness can diminish and can be replaced with peace and comfort.

Praying can do more than bring us comfort—it can also provide us with direction. We should remember that when we pray we must be willing to follow the guidance we receive. There was a point in 2004 when Joel and I had been back and forth about what we should do to resolve our infertility. Artificial insemination had failed. I had one of my damaged fallopian tubes removed. We knew that hormone therapy was not needed, and we knew there was not anything wrong with Joel.

It seemed to us that we had four options: to wait to conceive naturally, to commit to the process of IVF, to adopt, or to rest assured that we would live a life with just the two of us. If we waited to conceive naturally, we might be waiting as long as Abraham and Sarah did. IVF seemed like a gamble because of the large amount of money involved and the significant possibility of failure. At that point, I was not interested in considering adoption because I, like many of you, wanted the experience of having a child within my womb, of enduring childbirth, and raising a child my husband and I had created. The option of living a life without children, although very sad, I could probably come to terms with, but at this particular time, I was not ready for that either.

One night, I knelt in prayer. I wanted to know if the procedure of IVF would be the best option for our situation or if we should allow time for the miracle of conceiving naturally. As I prayed, I began by asking if we should do IVF, but when I went to say "in vitro," my mind drew a blank. I could not come up with the name of the procedure that had been the topic of so many conversations in the recent past. After pausing, I then said "Or should I . . ." but before completing my phrase, I heard a voice that said, "Wait." I was overwhelmed by the stupor of thought and then the undeniable direction to simply "wait." At the time, I did not know how long my wait would be or what exactly I was waiting for. I was given an answer that was not what I expected, but it was a miraculous answer to a prayer. I would eventually come to learn that in waiting both disappointment and miracles would happen.

Elder Joseph B. Wirthlin said, "Without faith, our prayers are merely words. With faith, our prayers connect with the powers of heaven and can bring upon us increased understanding, hope, and power. If by faith the worlds were created, then by faith we can create and receive the righteous desires of our hearts."[3]

Invoke the Power of the Priesthood

Does invoking the power of the priesthood guarantee success? It truly depends on how you measure success. Priesthood blessings will tell you exactly what Heavenly Father wants to communicate to you and can bring the specific comfort and peace you need. Why not use this powerful tool?

I remember receiving priesthood blessings at the hands of loving bishops as they set me apart for callings. Knowing the sadness that permeated my heart, Heavenly Father inspired them to say words that indicated that the desires of my heart would someday be realized. I have held on to those promises given through the power of a loving Father.

Prior to each procedure during the process of our infertility treatments, Joel would pronounce a blessing upon my head that the procedure would go well and that the doctors would be able to perform according to the best of their ability. Did these blessings bring the miracle of conception? No, they did not. These blessings did allow for the expertise of various doctors and nurses to be used on my behalf; the abilities and knowledge of these medical professionals led to diagnoses and suggestions for treatment. These blessings again brought peace and comfort by helping me know that Heavenly Father was in control and aware of every small thing we were doing. How grateful I am for a husband who is worthy to hold the power and authority of God and to pronounce great blessings upon my head.

Use the Scriptures as a Companion

One of my favorite things about reading the scriptures is the sensory experience it gives me. Not only do the words that I read from the pages bring me comfort, peace, conviction, and direction, but the way scriptures smell, look, and feel brings a power into each day. I love holding my scriptures. I love opening the cover, the binding of which is creased and weakened. The once shiny silver lining on the edges of the pages is long gone. I find joy in thumbing through the pages; some are crisp and others are worn and well-marked. Some of my favorite pages are those that are marked more with my ink than the ink of the printing press. To me, coming upon the writing in the margins is like remembering a spiritual awakening I had the last time I read the passage.

Like a true friend, the scriptures influence me for the good. When I invite this friend into my life by actively studying and pondering, I am an improved person: I have a stronger desire *and* the courage to do what is right at *all* times; I feel like I have increased wisdom; and I am assured that when things go horribly wrong, my friend will be there to provide me with exactly what I need.

I have shared some scripture stories from the Bible that can bring strength. You can apply other scriptures to your personal struggle, but you have to read them to find their strength. As you read the scriptures, you may want to mark, in an identifying color, the scriptures that give you particular comfort as you deal with infertility. If you do so, you can open your scriptures at any time and flip to one of these scriptures for comfort. Here are only a few scriptural friends that have helped me:

- Doctrine & Covenants 11:14: "And then shall ye know, or by this shall you know, all things whatsoever you desire of me, which are pertaining unto things of righteousness, in faith believing in me that you shall receive."
- Alma 18:32: "Yea, and he looketh down upon all the children of men; and he knows all the thoughts and intents of the heart."
- Mormon 9:21: "Behold, I say unto you that whoso believeth in Christ, doubting nothing, whatsoever he shall ask the Father in the name of Christ it shall be granted him; and this promise is unto all, even unto the ends of the earth." My mom mentioned this scripture as one that she has visited several times during our struggle.

The words of the hymn "As I Search the Holy Scriptures" teach us quite vividly about the affect reading the scriptures can have upon us:

> As I search the holy scriptures,
> Loving Father of mankind,
> May my heart be blessed with wisdom,
> And may knowledge fill my mind.
>
> As I search the holy scriptures,
> Touch my spirit, Lord, I pray.
> May life's myst'ries be unfolded
> As I study day by day.
>
> As I search the holy scriptures,
> May thy mercy be revealed.
> Soothe my troubled heart and spirit;
> May my unseen wounds be healed.
>
> As I search the holy scriptures,
> Help me ponder and obey.
> In thy word is life eternal;
> May thy light show me the way.[4]

In the Book of Mormon, we are challenged to feast upon the words of Christ (see 2 Nephi 32:3). Consider this image of feasting. When I think of a feast, I think of consuming an abundance of food, even to the point of filling my body, and most important, relishing every delicious morsel. I think of devouring foods that I enjoy very much. When we physically feast, our bodies receive nourishment and energy to accomplish those tasks before us. We also sometimes feel like we are going to burst!

Likewise, feasting upon the word of God, by seeking, devouring, and relishing every morsel, gives energy to our spirits so we can be spiritually strong. Feasting upon the scriptures means we are filling our lives to overflowing by reading the scriptures purposefully, frequently, and with a desire to apply them to our lives. In return, we receive intense energy of the Spirit—energy that will give us greater capacity and perspective. Have you feasted so much upon the scriptures that you feel you could burst?

Feasting upon the scriptures will invite them to become your friend and companion. They will bring you closer to the Spirit and encourage a deepening of your discipleship. The scriptures can also facilitate miracles of greater wisdom and understanding, guidance, hope, and the healing of a saddened heart. I encourage you to re-read the scriptures and feast upon the words of our current Church leaders. Prayerfully consider how the messages you read can specifically help you with the real, and often intense, suffering of infertility. They may not talk specifically about infertility, but so much of what we read can be applied specifically. I promise that as you read, inviting the Spirit to open your eyes, your spirit will receive great strength, and you will be surprised how many scriptures penetrate your heart and bring the healing feelings of peace.

Increase Your Faith

On my road of infertility, I have felt that my faith has been exhausted. In fact, there have been times that I wanted to ask Heavenly Father why He was not recognizing my faith. After all, I was praying, going to church, serving in my calling, fasting, and attending the temple. I have learned that it is essential to spiritual survival to be constantly cultivating faith, even if our faith seems to go unnoticed. Our faith can be expanded as we believe and repeatedly choose to live obediently. Elder David S. Baxter taught us that "faith is like spiritual oxygen. As we allow faith to freely flow within us, it awakens and enlivens our spiritual senses. It breathes life into our very souls. As faith flows, we become sensitively attuned to the whisperings of the Spirit. Our minds are enlightened, our spiritual pulse quickens, our hearts are touched."[5]

Faith can transform us because the Spirit is more abundantly with us when we have faith. Faith changes our perspectives, gives meaning to our lives, and destroys despair.

Recently, Joel and I decided that we needed to do an inventory of our faithfulness and the level of our discipleship; after all, there must be some ways our spiritual senses could be enlivened. We sat down one Sunday evening to discuss what we could do to increase our faith. I do not feel that we were faithless prior to the discussion, but I thought we needed to take inventory of our busy lives on the plateau of comfort and find some ways to start climbing again. We inventoried our scripture study, prayers, fasting, and temple attendance. We could have evaluated our family home evenings, how we serve in our callings, what we do to help other people, and many other things, but we did not want to overwhelm ourselves. We spent several months improving our scripture study, committing to petitioning our Heavenly Father more sincerely, fasting with greater intent, and seeking the Spirit in the temple.

I encourage you to sit down with your spouse and determine specific things you can do to increase your faith. I cannot adequately express the difference these changes made in my personal life and in my marriage. My trials did not disappear. I did, however, see small yet significant miracles: the feeling of greater joy in my life, an increased desire to absorb the teachings of the scriptures, an increased closeness to the Spirit, and an increase in the quality of my prayers (I actually *talk* to Heavenly Father and *discuss* things with Him). Additionally, I received strength as I served in my calling, I noticed a deeper love for my husband, and I felt a greater capacity to endure the challenges we faced together. What a difference it made. I truly felt my spiritual pulse quickened.

Do an inventory of your faith. Decide what you can do to get off of the plateau you are on. Start climbing again.

Go to the Mountain of the Lord

The temple is a quiet place where we can communicate soul to soul with our Savior and our Heavenly Father. The temple is a sanctuary for the soul, providing a place of spiritual refuge. It is a place of learning where the Holy Ghost teaches us about eternity and how our life on earth has eternal significance. We can receive personal direction when answers are found no where else. The temple reminds us of our purpose in life, emphasizes the promised blessings that are ours as we keep our covenants, renews our perspective, and allows us to see the Lord's hand in our lives. By enhancing our temple experiences, we can see these blessings adorn our lives more abundantly. Elder L. Lionel Kendrick suggested several things we can do to have "a rich spiritual experience" in the temple:

- "While in the temple we should act as if we are in His holy presence."
- "We should respond to His invitation [to come to the temple] by being worthy, by being prepared, and by having the temple as a priority in our lives."
- We should be reverent. Reverence "involves an awareness of what is taking place. It involves a divine desire to learn and to be receptive to the promptings of the Spirit. It involves a striving to seek added light and knowledge."
- "We must leave the world behind."
- "Our thoughts should be spiritual in nature."
- "We should also leave our worldly discussions behind."[6]

I have gone to the temple with a heavy but prayerful heart, hoping that I would receive heavenly direction. I have vivid memories of when, in response to my petition, things were revealed to me in the temple. These revelations were not earth shattering, and no one in the room knew of their occurrence, but to me, they were significant—they were spiritual "aha!" moments. I have participated in the temple ordinances numerous times, but in these moments of revelation, it seemed as though I was hearing them for the first time. I can remember feelings of over-whelming awe as I recognized that the Spirit had communicated directly with me; there was no doubt that my soul's complaint had been heard. In these quiet awakenings, my understanding of adversity changed, my life felt acceptable, peace encircled me, and I simply felt content. I knew that Heavenly Father was mindful of me. Isaiah 2:3 says, "Come ye, and let us go up to the mountain of the Lord, to the house of the God of Jacob; and he will teach us of his ways, and we will walk in his paths."

Let us enhance our lives by going to the temple. Through personal revelation within the temple, we can know of His ways for us personally and we can be recommitted to walking in His paths amid the challenges we face.

Enjoy the Blessings of the Atonement of Our Savior Jesus Christ

One of my favorite hymns is "I Know That My Redeemer Lives." The second verse reminds me of how the Savior *knows* my feelings. The words poetically read:

> He lives to comfort me when faint.
> He lives to hear my soul's complaint.
> He lives to silence all my fears.
> He lives to wipe away my tears.
> He lives to calm my troubled heart.
> He lives all blessings to impart.[7]

It is because of the Atonement that Christ can comfort, hear, silence, calm, and bless us when our lives are troubled. In fact, one of the fruits of the Atonement is Christ's ability to succor His people.

Alma taught the people of Gideon (and us) the principle of succoring: "And he will take upon him death, that he may loose the bands of death which bind his people; and he will take upon him their infirmities, that his bowels may be filled with mercy, according to the flesh, that he may know according to the flesh how to succor his people according to their infirmities" (Alma 7:12). To succor means "to run to the aid of, to assist in times of distress, to relieve."

In Nazareth, His childhood home, Christ spoke among people who knew Him as a carpenter's son. He read a passage from the book of Isaiah that prophesied the Son of God would come to "heal the brokenhearted, to preach deliverance to the captives. . . . to set at liberty them that are bruised" (Luke 4:18). Of course, when Christ told them that He was the Son of God and that He would fulfill the prophesy, accomplishing the very things of which Isaiah testified, the people doubted Him, were unbelieving and upset, and threw him out of the city. But what a powerful message He proclaimed: He would "heal the brokenhearted . . . set at liberty them that are bruised." I know I have felt bruised. I have felt injured, yet there is no outward physical sign of the damage done. To others, my body looks fine. They would never be suspicious that inside my soul is tender and aching. The scriptures teach, however, that through Christ, peace is assured. As I apply the Atonement in my life, through Christ, I am promised freedom from my sorrow and pain.

All my life, I have been taught "to apply the Atonement," but I can't remember anyone ever really teaching me what that meant. Yes, I knew that I could progress through the process of repentance and be forgiven for sins and shortcomings, but how could I "apply the Atonement" to ease my pains and sufferings? Was I not listening during a Sunday School lesson, not understanding a family home evening lesson, or was I never taught the specifics of how to apply the Atonement? Now as an adult woman (I am ashamed to admit it), when the revelation came, I realized that I knew it all along. The process is so simple! As I read the *Preach My Gospel* manual published by the Church for missionary work, I learned that to apply the Atonement "we must show that we accept [Christ] and that we will follow His commandments." In return, "He can help us endure our trials, sicknesses, and pain. We can be filled with joy, peace, and consolation. All that is unfair about life can be made right through the Atonement of Jesus Christ."[8]

It clicked. In order for me to receive the peace of Jesus Christ that I so desperately needed, and if I wanted Him to run to my aid, I needed to demonstrate in word, thought, and deed that I would follow the commandments and accept Him. Accepting Him meant that I would need to follow in His ways, do all that He has asked, and become like Him. Now, with this tangible understanding, I could create a checklist of specific things I could do to approach the Savior. Instead of departing from Him or leaving Him because I was filled with sorrow and felt forgotten, I could consciously move toward Him.

My life has been richly blessed by Elder Jeffrey R. Holland's explanation of how Christ can assist us when we feel bruised, brokenhearted, and powerless:

> I speak to those who are facing personal trials and family struggles, those who endure conflicts fought in the lonely foxholes of the heart,

those trying to hold back floodwaters of despair that sometimes wash over us like a tsunami of the soul. I wish to speak particularly to you who feel your lives are broken, seemingly beyond repair.

To all such I offer the surest and sweetest remedy that I know. It is found in the clarion call the Savior of the world Himself gave. . . . "Come unto me, all ye that labour and are heavy laden, and I will give you rest. . . . Ye shall find rest unto your souls."[9]

Because of the Atonement, Christ knows the trouble of my heart. Because He felt my sorrows, He is the only one who knows how to adequately comfort me. I know that if I "come unto [Him]," He will understand and hear the complaints of my soul, wipe away my tears of disappointment, and silence my fears of the unknown. The Savior *knows* your feelings, too. He wants to run to your aid and relieve your pain. He wants to strengthen you and to fix that which is broken in your lives such that you "might have life, and that [you] might have it more abundantly" (John 10:10).

> In Nazareth, the narrow road,
> That tires the feet and steals the breath,
> Passes the place where once abode
> The Carpenter of Nazareth.
>
> And up and down the dusty way
> The village folk would often wend;
> And on the bench, beside Him, lay
> Their broken things for Him to mend.
>
> The maiden with the doll she broke,
> The woman with the broken chair,
> The man with broken plough, or yoke,
> Said, "Can you mend it, Carpenter?"
>
> And each received the thing he sought,
> In yoke, or plough, or chair, or doll;
> The broken thing which each had brought
> Returned again a perfect whole.
>
> So, up the hill the long years through,
> With heavy step and wistful eye,
> The burdened souls their way pursue,
> Uttering each the plaintive cry:

"O Carpenter of Nazareth,
This heart, that's broken past repair,
This life, that's shattered nigh to death,
Oh, can You mend them, Carpenter?"

And by His kind and ready hand,
His own sweet life is woven through
Our broken lives, until they stand
A New Creation—"all things new."

"The shattered [substance] of [the] heart,
Desire, ambition, hope, and faith,
Mould Thou into the perfect part,
O, Carpenter of Nazareth!"[10]

The Atonement is an enabling power—it makes weak things strong and allows us to become whole. Through Jesus Christ, we can find the strength to move forward even when all seems hopeless. Because of Him we can be empowered to progress towards becoming what Heavenly Father sees we can be. Additionally, applying the atoning power in our lives will bring much needed healing and relief.

Notes

1. "Communicate," Dictionary.com, *The American Heritage Dictionary of the English Language*, Fourth Edition (Houghton Mifflin Company, 2004), http://dictionary.reference.com/browse/communicate.
2. Spencer W. Kimball, "Pray Always," *Ensign*, Oct. 1981, 3.
3. Joseph B. Wirthlin, "Improving Our Prayers, *Ensign*, Mar. 2004, 27.
4. "As I Search the Holy Scriptures," *Hymns*, no. 277.
5. David S. Baxter, "Faith, Service, Constancy," *Ensign*, Nov. 2006, 13.
6. L. Lionel Kendrick, "Enhancing Our Temple Experience," *Ensign*, May 2001, 78, 79.
7. "I Know That My Redeemer Lives," *Hymns*, no. 136.
8. *Preach My Gospel* (Salt Lake City: The Church of Jesus Christ of Latter-day Saints, 2004), 52.
9. Jeffrey R. Holland, "Broken Things to Mend," *Ensign*, May 2006, 69).
10. George Blair, "The Carpenter of Nazareth," as quoted in Holland, "Broken Things to Mend," 71.

CHAPTER ELEVEN

Strategies for Your Mind

Much of the way we act is a product of our education, the thoughts that posses our minds, and our ability to reason with and react well to life's situations. The ideas I suggest in this chapter include ways to keep your mind focused on the things that will move you forward rather than on those things that will weigh you down in the mire of self-pity.

Remember Your Individual Worth

Don't forget that you are more than your infertility. Although it is hard to stop labeling yourself as broken or defective, it is an important part of recognizing that your identity is defined by much more than your inability to conceive and bear children. Your worth as an individual is not determined by your status as a mother. Take your mind back to the Young Women values. The third one in line, but not third in importance, is individual worth. We learn in Young Women classes that each woman is "of infinite worth with [her] own divine mission, which [she] will strive to fulfill."[1]

Each woman has her own divine mission—a mission from Heavenly Father. Our success in life will be judged on accomplishing that mission, not on our ability to conceive children. Heavenly Father will not compare you to your sister, your friend, or the neighbor down the street. He will judge you according to your divine potential and who you have the capacity to become. That means we better be working on our whole selves, not just on conceiving and bearing children. You have other roles to fulfill. You can be a terrific wife, a compassionate sister, a caring friend, a thoughtful daughter, a successful businesswoman, a great skier, an exciting Primary teacher, a trusted Young Women leader. Happiness can be found as you find success in these roles as well. Celebrate that you have other parts of yourself that are functional and keep track of the context of your whole self, your whole life, and not just the narrow window of infertility.

Elder Russell M. Nelson said:

> I honor women who are not mothers. They know that motherhood is but one of the realms of womankind. The virtue and intelligence of women are uniquely applicable to other realms as well, such as compassionate service and teaching. . . .
>
> Her self-esteem cannot be based on physical features, possession or lack of a particular talent, or comparative quantities of anything. Her self-esteem is earned by individual righteousness and a close relationship with God. Her outward glow is generated by goodness within. And her patience is much more apparent than any imperfection. (See D&C 67:13) . . .
>
> Feelings of worth come when a woman follows the example of the Master. Her sense of infinite worth comes from her own Christlike yearning to reach out with love, as He does.[2]

I love that! It makes me want to work more on following the Master than on anything else.

Keep a Journal

Write your thoughts down. I am trying to be better about this element of life. I admit that I am better than my husband—his journal doesn't even know we got married.

Why should you write down your thoughts? Let's count some of the reasons:

- You can see the growth and the progress you have made.
- You can document where you have been and who you have become. Trust me, you will want to look back and remember. When you want to remember, your mind will fail you, but the words you shared in ink will bring it to your remembrance.
- Writing your feelings can be therapeutic. The process of

thinking and then writing (or even just writing without thinking) helps you work through emotions and see what you truly feel. According to Alexandra Johnson in *Leaving a Trace*, "journals are about sharpening consciousness."[3]

- Journaling helps you focus a multitude of thoughts, wishes, and sorrows by bringing them in like a net that brings in hundreds of fish. It is "a rare activity centered in the present, contemplating the past, yet aimed for a future self. . . . Journal writing is, foremost, a way to order and reframe perspective."[4]
- In a journal you can express the truest feelings within your heart, the ones you are too afraid to share with others. "Journals [are] the private place where the public mask [can] drop."[5]
- You will not be judged by what you write in your journal.
- It will be easier to identify ways the Lord is blessing you. President Eyring suggested sitting down each day and thinking of all the ways the Lord has blessed you. He said "Before I would write, I would ponder this question: 'Have I seen the hand of God reaching out to touch us or our children or our family today?' As I kept at it, something began to happen. As I would cast my mind over the day, I would see evidence of what God had done for one of us that I had not recognized in the busy moments of the day. As that happened, and it happened often, I realized that trying to remember had allowed God to show me what He had done."[6]

I have often looked back at my journal entries and thought I was the most depressing person. For years, from the way things read, I don't think I ever wrote in my journal on a happy day. Pathetic and rather embarrassing! I believe that a journal is a place to convey thoughts that you might not share with anyone else; it is a place where your feelings and thoughts find refuge; and it is a place where you can dump thoughts in an effort to make sense of them. For a majority of my life, my journal has not been that; my journal needed an overhaul. I wanted my journal to be a place where I shared my feelings constructively, and I wanted journal writing to become therapeutic. Additionally, I wanted my words to be helpful to me and perhaps others in the future.

In an effort to improve my journaling, I knew I needed to move away from repetitive apologies for failing to keep current followed by a bulleted list recounting *everything* that had happened since my last entry. I also wanted to stop considering my journal as a place for negative feelings only, but rather, pages filled with things I thought about: the good and bad as well as the interesting and mundane.

I believe that journaling becomes more meaningful when we move beyond a journal that is a travel log to one that is a record of our lives, experiences, relationships, feelings, and ideas. As I am trying to change my journaling perspective, I find that my journal beckons me to write and it provides me with a place of refuge and thinking. Yes, I write in my journal about the unfairness of my life. But I also write about things I observe in others and in myself. I write about my experiences with people and in the world. I enjoy searching for things that spark thoughts in my mind and then write about them. It might be a lesson in Sunday School, a story on the news, an experience as I serve in a calling, a scripture I read, or something that happens at the grocery store. If it is worthy of my thinking, it is certainly worthy of recording. My goal is to capture little moments in my life so that in a future day, I can read about it in my journal and remember it vividly.

Because of my newfound desire to write more frequently, handwriting my words was too time consuming and limited my ability to expand on thoughts. To solve the problem, I began typing my journal. Sure, gone are the days of feeling a personal connection with handwritten words as I flip through the pages of my journal and gone are the days of buying really neat journals that invite me to write in them. But, because of my change in journaling, I feel an increased urgency to write my thoughts down.

I am impressed by what President Spencer W. Kimball said,

> Your private journal should record the way you face up to challenges that beset you. . . . Experiences of work, relations with people, and an awareness of the rightness and wrongness of actions will always be relevant. Your journal, like most others, will tell of problems as old as the world and how you dealt with them.
>
> Your journal should contain your true self rather than a picture of you when you are "made up" for a public performance. There is a

temptation to paint one's virtues in rich color and whitewash the vices, but there is also the opposite pitfall of accentuating the negative. . . .

Your journal is your autobiography, so it should be kept carefully. You are unique, and there may be incidents in your experience that are more noble and praiseworthy in their way than those recorded in any other life. . . .

What could you do better . . . than to record the story of your life, your triumphs over adversity, your recovery after a fall, your progress when all seemed black, your rejoicing when you had finally achieved? . . .

Begin today and write in it your goings and your comings, your deeper thoughts, your achievements, and your failures, your associations and your triumphs, your impressions and your testimonies . . . those who keep a personal journal are more likely to keep the Lord in remembrance in their daily lives.[7]

You can even have an "inspirational thought" journal in which you keep the quotes, scriptures, lyrics, hymns, poems, and talks by Church leaders that mean something to you. Whenever I review the thoughts I write in my journal of "Things That Mean Something to Me," I am granted a small piece of wisdom that seems to carry me forward. Here are some thoughts from my journal:

"When filled with God's love, we can do and see and understand things that we could not otherwise do or see or understand. Filled with His love, we can endure pain, quell fear, forgive freely, avoid contention, renew strength, and bless and help others in ways surprising even to us."[8] *In this quote, Elder Groberg gives me a checklist—I love checklists! Here, he tells me a specific way for my life to be blessed with things I desire. By filling myself with the love of God I can overcome and endure. Our capacity to accomplish great things increases and our spiritual vision changes as our hearts become like His.*

"I know some of you do truly feel at sea, in the most frightening sense of that term. . . . It is not without a recognition of life's tempests but fully and directly because of them that I testify of God's love and the Savior's power to calm the storm. . . . Christ knows better than all others that the trials of life can be very deep and we are not shallow people if we struggle with them. But . . . He rebukes faithlessness and He deplores pessimism. He expects us to believe!"[9] *Infertility has made me feel at sea. It has caused me to feel tempest-tossed, frightened, and very much alone. As I choose to believe in Christ's ability to save me from the tragedies of storms, I prove not only my depth of discipleship, but my faith that He loves and cares for me individually. By exercising such faith, I enable Him to calm my storms.*

"When we worry about the future, we create unhappiness in the present. Righteous concern may lead us to take appropriate action, but worrying about things we cannot control can paralyze and demoralize us."[10] *I have felt the paralysis of being demoralized by the unhappiness I create when I worry obsessively about my infertility. I have learned that it is important to recognize when our concern turns from righteous worrying to all-consuming distress.*

"May you live all the days of your life."[11] *There shouldn't be a day I regret. Despite unfulfilled expectations, I can consciously choose to fill each day with purpose and meaning. I want to be productive. I want to be filled with life.*

Commit to revitalizing your journaling. Decide how you can make it meaningful and therapeutic for you personally. Allow it to be a way to process your feelings while you preserve meaningful thoughts and experiences. Let your journal become a friend and a confidante.

Educate Yourself and Then Others

One day I went to a local bookstore to see what resources were available on infertility. I was a bit disappointed by the store's selection of only six or seven titles. As I flipped through the books, I saw diagrams of the female and male anatomy and an explanation of how conception occurs. My first thought: "I'm pretty sure we grasp how conception works—high school biology provided us with that. Who do these 'experts' think we are? Do they think that the only people having fertility problems are idiots?"

There were, however, a couple of books that provided ample information on everything from finding a specialist to considering the ethics of fertility treatments to understanding the latest drugs available to dealing with pregnancy loss. My recommendation is to find a resource, whether it is a book, a website, a specialist, or a combination of all three, that can provide you with a good education. Make sure the sources are valid. Research from professional academies and medical associations are often most reliable. Ask Heavenly Father to help you discern truth and ethical behavior out of the resources you use.

Stay current on the latest information so that you know what your options are. Educating yourself will not only help you with the decisions you face but will be priceless as you communicate with others regarding infertility. You will be able to explain causes, treatments, medications, and processes with greater ease.

When my husband and I began telling our families about our infertility, we did a great deal of explaining. Since we do not have Relief Society activities on infertility (and I am not saying we should), many people do not know much, if anything, about infertility. We educated our parents and some of our siblings about infertility treatments. I think we taught our parents more than they ever wanted to know about the reproductive system.

You never know when the topic of fertility issues will come up in conversation, whether at a home teaching or visiting teaching appointment, at a ward party, or in a Sunday School lesson. If you educate yourself, you will be ready to act with valuable information.

Remember: "Seek ye diligently and teach one another words of wisdom; yea, seek ye out of the best books words of wisdom; seek learning, even by study and also by faith" (D&C 88:118).

Be Filled with Gratitude

A noted clinical psychologist, Jon Spiegel said that "in practicing gratitude, we defy despair."[12]

Epicurus said, "Don't spoil what you have by desiring what you have not; but remember that what you now have was once among the things only hoped for."

Elder J. Reuben Clark said: "Hold fast to the blessings which God has provided for you. Yours is not the task to gain them; yours is the part of cherishing them."[13]

Finally, President Howard W. Hunter admonished us, "I think it is incumbent upon us to rejoice a little more and despair a little less, to give thanks for what we have and for the magnitude of God's blessings to us, and to talk a little less about what we may not have."[14]

I could continue to quote great people who have encouraged us to show gratitude. Why? What does gratitude do that changes us so much? Gratitude changes our hearts and helps us to see with new eyes—spiritual eyes. As we look for greater understanding about this process, let us look first at what gratitude is not. Gratitude is not an attitude of pessimism. When we are pessimistic, we complain and are critical of every little thing. We tend to overlook that which is significant as we blame and point fingers. Pessimism is destructive to our minds and spirits, our perspectives, and ultimately to our relationship with the Savior.

While pessimism destroys, gratitude creates. It creates within us an ability to be filled with joy, love, understanding, and appreciation. It changes how we perceive the world and even how we see our own lives. Simply stated, gratitude enlarges the soul. By recognizing and acknowledging that we have been abundantly blessed, we can become at peace with our lives and enjoy an elevated capacity to endure "all things wherewith [we] have been afflicted" (D&C 98:3). Our capacity to endure changes because gratitude "turns our own hearts toward the Savior. . . . We develop Christlike characteristics, such as humility and unselfishness, to offset tendencies to be prideful, selfish, and unforgiving. . . .

"Thankfulness frequently expressed through prayer, testimony, conversation, and living the gospel reflects a spiritual maturity that exists in people who are truly grateful."[15]

Is it not amazing that our gratitude can be expressed simply by the way we live?

Infertility can cause feelings of pessimism. It is easy to complain. It is also easy to overlook the fact that life is happening despite infertility. Other things are taking place—other things to be grateful for. I have tried to make it a habit to identify something each week to be grateful for. I have found gratitude in a talk or lesson someone presented at church, a compliment someone made to me, the warmth of sun that gives life and light to the earth, or the words of a song. I have tried to write more thank-you notes to those who have been the subject of my gratitude. It is easy to get caught up in the negativity of trials. But it is also easy to be caught up in the spirit of gratitude, if we choose. This spirit of gratitude is what changes our perspective and our spiritual vision.

Celebrate

The quest for a successful pregnancy can involve a long, winding road with more than a few bumps, potholes, and maybe even a few 180-degree turns. This quest may last six months, ten years, or even longer. To remain sane, celebrate every once in a while. We all need an excuse for a dinner out, a bowl of vanilla bean ice cream with raspberries and chocolate sauce (one of my favorites), or a trip to a favorite place. Decide with your spouse when you will celebrate. Is there a reason to celebrate? Of course there is. Will it be when you find out the reason for your infertility? Will it be on the anniversary of when you started fertility treatments? Will it be on the day you find out you are pregnant? Will it be when you keep yourself from speaking unkindly about a friend who just announced she is pregnant with baby number three? Or will it be every day as you recognize the great blessing of having a wonderful and understanding spouse? Celebrating can make the journey seem bearable. It allows you and your spouse time to reflect on where you have been and where you are going. It also helps you keep perspective. With infertility, you are experiencing extraordinary challenges every day—so celebrate!

Not long ago, my husband and I went to one of our favorite places—Las Vegas. I have not been able to figure out why this is one of our favorite places because so much of it is full of filth and sleaze. I have a feeling it may be our favorite place because it was the first place we spent a vacation just the two of us since our honeymoon (five years too late!). Or maybe it is because the fountains at the Bellagio Hotel hold a magical power over us. Who knows?

Anyway, while we were there for a friend's wedding, we went to a specialty store on the Las Vegas Strip and purchased our favorite bubbling soda in a glass bottle. We decided that because the beverage looked like a collector's item and very special, we would save it to be consumed for a special occasion. Having our fertility issues on my mind, I said, "We should drink it on the day we find out we are pregnant." Joel agreed. And both of us wondered how much dust would collect on the bottle before we would open it—if we ever did open it. A small, silly celebration like this could quench an incredible thirst!

As we all know, infertility has a way of making life peculiar and not quite "normal." I remember a time when I was driven to celebrate the eccentricity of my life. Several years ago, my husband's parents began a new Christmas tradition. They decided to take the whole family to a popular one-stop shopping location, give everyone a lump sum of cash, and then let us loose. During the hour-long spree, we each scour the store determining exactly which items were worthy of our impulse spending opportunity. Whatever we chose would be considered a generous Christmas gift from Grandma and Grandpa Daynes. The perfect family Christmas tradition, you might say!

The year we started this tradition, Joel and I were in the midst of infertility procedures, surgeries, and many unknowns—I was exhausted and was feeling miffed that my life was not going according to my plan. As I searched high and low for the perfect items to splurge on, I determined that it was absolutely needful that I celebrate the unconventional nature of my life with eccentric things. I chose to purchase a movie about a woman who defied the norms imposed by society. Additionally, I felt compelled to purchase *Stargirl* by Jerry Spinelli, a book that celebrates nonconformity. I know they say that you can't judge a book by its cover, but the cover of this book was so distinctly different that I was instantly drawn to it. Next, new pillows for our bed (and not the decorative kind) made their way into my cart. I felt assured that no one gets pillows for Christmas, thus they were perfect for my celebration. And finally, instead of blowing the remainder of my allotted cash, it made its way into our savings account, something *very* eccentric for me.

Weird. Yes. Silly. Yes. But a celebration nonetheless. Somehow this unusual demonstration made my infertility seem not so depressing and not so hopeless. In the end, I quite enjoyed the movie, the book made me smile, the pillows were so comfy, and my bank account appreciated the boost.

Wouldn't enduring doctor's visit after doctor's visit be more bearable if you planned to get a 99-cent hot fudge sundae after each one? Talk to your spouse and figure out how you will celebrate the milestones and victories along the way. Celebrating demonstrates gratitude for what you have, changes your perspective, and gives you motivation to keep going.

Notes

1. *Young Women Personal Progress: Standing as a Witness of God* (booklet, 2001), 26.
2. Russell M. Nelson, "Woman—Of Infinite Worth," *Ensign*, Nov. 1989, 20.
3. Alexandra Johnson, *Leaving a Trace: On Keeping a Journal* (Boston: Little, Brown and Company, 2001), 33.
4. Ibid., 31, 33.
5. Ibid., 32–33.
6. Henry B. Eyring, "O Remember, Remember," *Ensign*, Nov. 2007, 67.
7. Spencer W. Kimball, "President Kimball Speaks Out on Personal Journals," *Ensign*, Dec. 1980, 61, emphasis added.
8. John H. Groberg, "The Power of God's Love," *Ensign*, Nov. 2004, 11.
9. Jeffrey R. Holland, "'An High Priest of Good Things to Come,'" *Ensign*, Nov. 1999, 36–37.
10. Joseph B. Wirthlin, "Improving Our Prayers," *Ensign*, Mar. 2004, 28.
11. Jonathan Swift, *Polite Conversation* (London: Chiswick Press), 154.
12. In Ann Rodgers, "Feeling Troubled? Try a Little Gratitude," *Pittsburgh Post-Gazette*, November 23, 2006.
13. *Church News*, June 14, 1969, 2.
14. Howard W. Hunter, *That We Might Have Joy* (Salt Lake City: Deseret Book, 1994), 92–93.
15. "The Visiting Teacher: 'More Gratitude Give Me,'" *Ensign*, July 1995, 70.

CHAPTER TWELVE

Social and Relational Strategies

Wouldn't it be nice to live in a bubble, insulated from our trials and the outside influences that aggravate wounds or bring up troubling thoughts? Of course, this is impossible, so it's helpful for couples dealing with infertility to find solutions to handle difficult social settings and everyday relationships with family and friends. Here are some suggestions that might help.

Enjoy Children

This one may sound unconventional, but read on. I think that infertility causes us to shy away from the very thing we cannot have—children. In our sadness, it is easy to isolate ourselves.

I am the second of four girls, and three of us are married. There are also three boys who complete the family. I was married first, followed three years later by my sister just younger than me, who was followed one-and-a-half years later by the youngest sister. The thing that is not quite fair is that Kim, the youngest of us girls, got pregnant and had a baby first. Is it *supposed* to work that way?

I figured that I could choose one of two reactions. I could be angry with my pregnant sister, or I could celebrate this exciting time with her. After all, I would want her to be excited about my pregnancy. I started by initiating a "congratulations gift" from all of us girls (including Mom). It made me feel a little better and got my mind off of the disappointment . . . for a short time. I made a conscious decision that I would not let the unfairness I saw to allow me to become bitter.

During the nine months of her pregnancy, Kim and I went on walks. We talked about what she was feeling. We talked about names. We talked about parenting. We went shopping for baby stuff (my favorite). I had so much fun. I am not saying it wasn't hard, because it was. However, at the same time, I saw that her happiness was bringing me happiness.

The night her son Nicholas was born, Joel and I dropped everything. We went to get another "congratulations gift" and hurried to the hospital. I cannot express the overwhelming happiness I felt as I saw my sister's son. I observed as her husband watched the nurse bathe him for the first time and as Nicholas had his first picture taken. I did not want to leave. I made plans to visit the following day during my lunch break.

Every time I was with Nicholas, I felt that longing for a child. Unexpectedly, however, it was bearable. I delighted in him and could not get enough of him. I probably annoyed my sister and brother-in-law because I always wanted to hold him, play with him, change his diaper, talk, and sing to him. I remember the day I was holding him and asked him if he knew any of his cousins in heaven—and if there were any waiting to join my family. At that moment, he stopped moving, looked directly in my eyes, and smiled. To me, this was a remarkable answer of things to come. He brought me great hope.

I still enjoy Nicholas. He enjoys going on walks with his mom and Aunt Kerstin. He enjoys coming to play at my home. He even enjoys me singing to him. I believe that if I had chosen to resent my sister because she was pregnant and I was not, I would have missed out on all of this.

Older children can bring happiness as well. I used to work at a preschool in a predominantly LDS community. Despite the natural times of frustration, the children brought joy into my life. They amazed me with their miraculous development, their innocence, their trust, and their unconditional love.

I remember the day when Caleb (age four) came into my office at the preschool. He leaned up against the door frame, looked me straight in the eye, pointed to me, and said with conviction like I have never seen before, "Kerstin, you are a child of God." I could not help but smile. Not too many days later, Caleb was deflated and disappointed because no one in class would sing "I Am a Child of God" with him.

On another day, my friend Tristan (age five) gave me a picture he had drawn. When I asked him to tell me about his creation, he pointed to a figure in the drawing and identified it as himself. I then asked him who the other two people in the drawing were. He indicated, quite matter-of-factly, that it was me and my son. Despite having no knowledge about my family and certainly not knowing my sorrows of infertility, he offered a glimmer of hope. Perhaps someday I would have a son.

Children add meaning to our lives. They add perspective we are sometimes too blind to see. Allowing ourselves to have experiences with them can bring much needed joy.

Become Involved in the Least Likely Places

Dr. Beth Cooper-Hilbert explained that "infertile women often talk about how encounters with groups of mothers make them feel isolated, like second-class citizens, unable to contribute or participate in the 'in-group.' "[1]

Sometimes it feels as though we live on the social periphery. But just because you do not have children does not mean you lack an understanding of them. Even though you are not a mother, you have still inherited the divine ability to nurture—you have great things to contribute to the lives of children. Does this mean you can nurture only your own children? No. You can nurture someone else's child, you can nurture a friend, you can nurture your spouse, you can nurture anyone. You *can* be part of the "in-group." I admire Sister Sheri Dew for her powerfully honest and heartfelt way of teaching and sharing. She wisely said, "For reasons known to the Lord, some women are required to wait to have children. This delay is not easy for any righteous woman. But the Lord's timetable for each of us does not negate our nature. Some of us, then, must simply find other ways to mother. And all around us are those who need to be loved and led."[2]

I have often thought that maybe Heavenly Father is giving me an extended period to master the skill of nurturing; by the time I have children I could be nearly perfect at this skill! Even though I say this as a way to make myself feel better, I think there is truth in it. You can use this time to become a proficient nurturer. Look for opportunities to use this talent. If it might seem a little hidden, hunt it down and find ways to keep it visible.

Elder Russell M. Nelson said, "Nurturing the young, comforting the frightened, protecting the vulnerable, teaching and giving encouragement need not—and should not—be limited to our own children."[3]

Many organizations focus their efforts on helping children. The CASA—Court Appointed Special Advocate—program needs volunteers to be advocates for children who have been abused. Jeremy Boyle and Stephen F. Duncan of "Forever Families" suggested some other ideas of places to get involved: "Elementary schools need volunteers to help children learn reading skills. Big Brothers and Big Sisters is always in need of adult mentors for teenagers. The Girl or Boy Scouts and community sports teams always need volunteers."[4] You may be able to change a life that no one else could. It is important to choose places to get involved.

It seems that many functions within the Church are "family friendly"—ward parties, Sunday School lessons, Relief Society activities, not to mention Mother's and Father's Day. You may say, "Why should I go? It will not apply to me," or "It will just make me sad and want children more," or "It will make me upset at those who have what I do not." It is sometimes easier to avoid social situations that may be uncomfortable.

Yes, you can *choose* to isolate yourself, but consider this: Dr. Cooper-Hilbert found that women who tend to "react with avoidant social behavior rather then engaging social behavior become vulnerable."[5]

Your situation can actually worsen when you choose not to engage or participate. Let's switch the response to "Why shouldn't I go? I want to see what I can learn. I may have something to share from my perspective." That sounds more confident and more proactive. It sounds like a can-do attitude. And it will change your countenance a bit.

During the warm spring, summer, and fall months, my neighborhood has play groups. The mothers in the area bring their children to play and socialize while they have adult conversation and an occasional treat. I decided that I would show up one day. Was I out of place? Perhaps only because I did not bring a child with me. Did the other women tell me to leave? No. Did they talk about their children? Only for 75 percent of the time. I had adult conversations with the other women, I smiled, and I played on the slide with my miniature friends from the ward (one of them even talked with me about going to the temple to get married to him). I bet no one expected me to show up, but I did, and I had a wonderful time. When I left, I was probably the only one who did not have to go home and put a child down for a nap.

Oftentimes young couples are called to be nursery leaders in their ward. Some of you may have had this experience. You may have wondered why you were called to care for someone else's children while you are deeply saddened by your inability to have your own. To you, the nursery may be the worst place to be. To Heavenly Father, the nursery may be where He needs you most. He sees your ability to love children and wants you to use it in teaching the young children in His kingdom here on earth.

I recently organized an Relief Society activity for my sister's ward. The title was "Tickle Every Sense: Fostering Creativity in Young Children." A woman who is single or without child may see the advertisements and say, "Well, that does not apply, so I am not going to go." That saddens me. Refusing experiences by being determined that it does not apply to you, or that it is just for people who are married and have children, is sentencing yourself to a life of misery and forfeiting friendships and opportunities to share your experience with others. Now, that may sound harsh. I do know that some women cannot bring themselves to be involved in such activities, but I encourage you to try it every once in a while and ask for the help of the Spirit. Go with a friend. You have a great deal of knowledge, wisdom, and experience that you can share with others. If you cannot make yourself go, accept that and set a goal to attend another time.

Establish a Network of Those Who Know

Few things are better than talking with someone who knows about the betrayal you feel from your body, the physical and emotional difficulties associated with infertility treatments, the loss of privacy, and the sadness. Talking with others who have experienced infertility will help you feel more normal. Knowing that someone else has experienced what you are feeling and then being able to share thoughts and feelings with that person can be one of the greatest gifts during the battle with infertility. As women, "we have to have a name for what we are experiencing and [know] that someone else has felt it."[6]

These friends hopefully know firsthand the importance of maintaining privacy and confidentiality. They are more likely to know which questions to ask and which not to ask. They know when to speak and when to listen. It is important to find others who can truly mourn with you and comfort you when you grieve. In turn, you can mourn with and comfort them. Remember as you choose to confide in your friends that you maintain the agreement you made with your spouse: How much will you share? How much will you keep quiet?

It is important to remember that having a friend who is experiencing infertility along with you may require that you celebrate when your friend triumphs. Will you be prepared emotionally to express sincere joy at her success? Remember that you would want her to truly celebrate your success.

I think we can find Sarah's response to the birth of her sweet and much anticipated son intriguing as we gain perspective about celebrating the success of others. After Isaac was born, the scriptures tell us that "Sarah said, God hath made me to laugh, so that all that hear will laugh with me" (Genesis 21:6). Now remember, to laugh in this context means to rejoice, which changes the meaning dramatically: "God hath made me to *rejoice*, so that all that hear will rejoice with me." It was indeed a miracle that Sarah had witnessed and she had every reason to rejoice and to be glad. Her story, filled with both sorrow and extreme joy, would likely give comfort, hope, and cause anyone who would hear it to rejoice. I am convinced that her story touched the lives of those around her just as much as it gives us reason to rejoice now, hundreds of years later. I can imagine that Sarah's daughter-in-law, Rebekah, and her granddaughter Rachel held onto the hope and faith of their matriarch to see them through their very personal struggles with being barren. Just as Sarah's rejoicing provides us reason to rejoice, every woman's successes during the struggle of being barren can also give us reason to rejoice.

I have several friends who are part of my "network." Some know the cause of their infertility, some are in the midst of treatments, while some are taking a much needed break. Others have found success in their quest for children while others have experienced repeated devastating disappointments. Some of my friends have experienced infertility for years and others are at the beginning of the road, just starting to wonder if there might be something wrong. My friends have provided me with listening ears. Those who have forged the way have guided my path and have provided me with an education of terms, procedures, and questions to ask. I have cried tears of sorrow with some friends and tears of joy with others. The setbacks have caused me to question certain procedures while the triumphs have given me courage to continue in faith.

I have found that a network provides not only emotional support but can also help build knowledge. These friends can assist you in

- finding a good specialist
- developing a list of questions to ask
- seeing the options you have
- staying abreast of new procedures
- locating financial resources
- and much more

Your network can be an invaluable resource to you.

Let me share some experiences I have had establishing my own network. Each one teaches a priceless lesson.

ANNA

I suspected that my cousin had been experiencing infertility for some time. The tip-off was cliché—she and her husband had been married for several years and had not had children. I wondered if breaking the silence may provide her some sort of comfort, but I knew I needed to treat the circumstance sensitively. Being in the same situation, I knew that I would have welcomed someone respectfully acknowledging my "problem" and validating my sorrow. I hoped that as I offered my love to her that she would see me as a resource and someone to talk to rather than a threat.

I decided to approach her privately at a family gathering. I prayed silently that I would express my feelings tenderly and be guided to say the exact thing she needed to hear. At the perfect moment, I approached her and pulled her aside. I said to her, "Anna, I have noticed that you and I have something in common, and I hope you are not offended by me bringing it up. I know that you and Nick have been married for some time and you have not yet had children." Once she confirmed my suspicion, I told her that I could imagine that her heart was hurting, because I knew that having children was the desire of her heart. I expressed my sadness for her. I assured her that if she had questions or wanted to share some of her feelings that I would be ready and willing to listen. I was not surprised when she was receptive; in fact, I sensed a feeling of relief. She spent a few moments sharing some of her thoughts.

This interchange alleviated some of the distress Anna was feeling. She was relieved to know that someone else actually *did* know the feelings she was having. At the time that I approached her, Anna and her husband were at the beginning of their journey with infertility. They were experiencing the feelings of being lost, confused, and betrayed. They were unsure about where to start. Opening the dialogue between us allowed Anna to comfortably ask questions about procedures, gave me the opportunity to make suggestions and share experiences, and permitted tears to flow freely. This relationship proved to be therapeutic for both of us.

MY TEMPLE FRIEND

Now, let me tell you about my temple friend. I call her my "temple friend" because I do not know her name and I could probably not pick her out of a crowd if I ever saw her again. But she has left a lasting impression on my heart. Joel and I went to the temple for a ward temple night. Our ward was planning on doing an endowment session, but because of circumstance, the time commitment would not work, so Joel and I decided to do sealings instead. When we inquired about sealings, we were told that we needed to be ready in three minutes. Time was of the essence! As I rushed back to the temple dressing room, I noticed a woman nervously and busily readying herself for sealings. Because it is always nice to have a companion when you are uncertain of where you need to go, I asked her if she wanted to figure out where we needed to be together. She agreed and we transported ourselves, with the help of a few nice temple workers, to the sealing office. During our venture, I learned several things about this woman: her nervousness was not a result of trying to get somewhere by a certain time, she did not make a lot of eye contact, she loved to talk, and she did not keep a whole lot secret.

When we found our husbands, we sat down, waited, and talked

quietly. To me, it seemed like this sister had not had anyone to talk to in a long time. I learned that after she had undergone several procedures to get pregnant, she had given birth to a set of twins, one of which was stillborn while the other one died two months later. She told me that she has several problems that complicate getting pregnant and maintaining a healthy pregnancy and that she felt like she will never be a mother. She seemed frustrated. She also indicated that she was not interested in doing IVF because it is not a guarantee of pregnancy and felt that just having a hysterectomy would solve a multitude of problems. She seemed hopeless. When there was a pause in the conversation, she asked about my family.

My first thought was, "Boy, won't you be surprised when you find out that I know a little something about how you feel?" It was when I mentioned that Joel and I had also experienced infertility that she began making eye contact. I briefly explained my story including that we had experienced several failed procedures, and that I knew the heavy heart and sorrow she was experiencing. She looked me directly in the eyes and said, "So you know exactly what I mean?" I told her "Yes, I know what you mean." At that moment, it was as if our understanding of sorrow connected us; our hearts shared something when our words could not. Unfortunately, the schedule of the temple could not wait for our conversation to end, and we were shuffled into separate sealing rooms.

During the sealing session, I could not help but wonder about this sweet acquaintance. I felt like our conversation had just begun and had so many places to go. Trying to focus on the task at hand, I put her in the back of my mind. After the session, Joel and I made our way back to the locker rooms. As I walked in, there she was! Her eyes beamed when she saw me, and she went on talking as if we had never been separated. During the next several minutes, I learned even more about her, but it seemed as though she had changed a bit.

Before we separated to go to different sealing rooms, I perceived that she was saddened by her health problems and was not encouraged by the prognosis. Upon meeting again, she seemed filled with greater hope. Instead of saying things such as "I don't think that will work . . ." or "We don't have a lot of options . . ." or even "I'm just going to have a hysterectomy so I don't have to worry about this . . .," she said "I think we are going to try . . .". I do not know what caused the change. Perhaps it was the Spirit of the temple. Perhaps it was simply knowing that someone else knew exactly how she felt. Perhaps it was a combination of both.

As we walked out of the temple that night together, she was smiling and so was I. We offered hope to each other as we said good-bye. I will probably never see her again, but I know there is hope in her future.

Kate

My third and final story is about Kate. My friendship with Kate began as visiting teaching companions. When we were assigned, I really did not really know a whole lot about her and her husband, and I would guess she knew little about me. In the beginning, I felt like we just were not connecting with each other and that we were not accomplishing what we needed to with our assigned sisters. I prayed that I would know what I could do to reach out to her, to improve the flow of conversation, to make her feel more comfortable around me, and to become her friend. Change did not happen overnight, but over time, something remarkable did happen.

I decided that I would try to notice the things that she brought up in conversations and then I would encourage conversations around those topics. In the process, I noticed two things: Kate loved children and Kate was looking forward to having children of her own. I also remember feeling that there was some tension regarding having a family.

One day after a visiting teaching appointment, we were walking home. On the corner where she would turn to go to her home and I would turn to go to my home, I felt impressed to ask her about this tension I perceived. I simply mentioned what I had observed in our conversations and offered a listening ear. Was my intention to get the dirt out of Kate because I was nosy? Not at all. My intention was pure—I wanted to be her friend. I cared about her and noticed that her heart was aching. I hoped that perhaps I could ease her burden in some way.

I learned a lot about my friend that day, but most of all, our relationship began to evolve. No longer did I feel that we were having forced conversations that were somewhat obligatory because of our callings. My heart began to love her, to be concerned for her, and to want the best for her.

I had no idea that my friendship with Kate would turn into an opportunity to share feelings about infertility. Not long after that day on the corner, Kate told me that she and her husband were experiencing some challenges with getting pregnant. After going through the not-so-fun tests, it was found that a couple of things were keeping her from conceiving. Of course she was frustrated, confused, saddened, and uncertain about what to do. Additionally, she did not feel like she was receiving the support she needed from her husband. As we shared a few moments together, I felt an almost tangible connection growing because our similar feelings of disappointment and sadness. It was almost as if our hearts were communicating. Neither one of us diminished the sorrow of the other, but rather, provided support and strength. Because I knew about the tests she was going through, I felt comfortable asking additional questions. I did not feel like an intrusive neighbor, but rather a friend who was truly concerned for her and her husband. And now, my prayers could take on a different dimension as I began to pray for her specific needs.

It was around this time that a "For Sale" sign went up on their lawn. I was disappointed that we were just beginning to develop this trusting relationship and now she would be moving! We all know that even with the best of intentions, it is hard to keep in touch with people once they have moved, so I did not have a lot of hope that this friendship would continue. Kate and her husband sold their home quickly and moved far enough away that they would no longer be in our ward or even our stake. Before they moved, I did learn that procedures and medicines were not working, that her husband was still not particularly open to being tested, and that she was frustrated that she often felt like she was in this quest on her own.

After they moved, I saw her once and talked to her a couple times on the phone. We had gone several months without talking, when I had begun thinking about her for a few weeks. However, I could not locate her phone number, so when she called me, I was thrilled! We chatted and spent some time getting caught up, and then I asked how things were with her health. I was secretly hoping that she was perhaps calling with the happy news of pregnancy, but she was not. Evidently, over the past several months of being on Clomid, nothing was happening, causing confusion and hopelessness. She knew that it was important that her husband be tested, had spent many unsuccessful months trying to convince him, and finally he agreed. Unfortunately, the results were not positive, but I could tell in her voice that regardless, this was a significant milestone. This was progress.

With additional answers, they began working with their doctor on different procedures that could increase their chances of pregnancy. She told me that she wanted to call and tell me because she knew I would be interested and would care about the progress they were making. Of course I cared! In fact, I was honored that she called me and her news thrilled me! They had answers, they had options, they had direction! I celebrated!

Do you see that my prayer had been answered? Heavenly Father paved the way for Kate and me to converse more freely, to understand each other better, to be comfortable around each other, and to ultimately become friends. Our assigned acquaintance blossomed into a relationship of trust, kindness, and sincere interest in each other's lives. It turned into an opportunity to share feelings and experiences. We both benefited.

Anna, Kate, and even my temple friend have taught me about the power of developing trusting relationships with those who share a common grief. In each of these stories, my friends experienced a sense of relief when a dialogue was opened and they were given freedom to express feelings that were overwhelming their hearts. Relief also came when they found out that someone else knew how they felt. They were grateful that someone actively made an effort to address the very thing they did not know how to reveal. They were craving a friend who would listen, could answer questions, and who could do it without passing judgment.

For many couples, healing can occur when they are approached tactfully about their infertility. Sometimes it is even better when a trusting relationship develops with someone else who is infertile. As we who are infertile proactively seek opportunities to open this dialogue, we can provide strength and support to others. Because we are in the midst of the sorrows, we can offer unique sensitivity and love that we know they need.

When you choose to approach someone about his or her infertility, think about these things:

- How would you appreciate being approached about your challenge with infertility?
- It is all too easy to diminish your friend's suffering by adding stories of others or switching the emphasis to you. Focus on her. Ask questions about her struggle. Add phrases such as "I can imagine that . . ." to communicate that you have had similar feelings.
- Before approaching your friend, review why are you asking him about infertility. Do you desire to offer support or are you just getting the scoop?
- Sometimes the discomfort of confrontation causes us to get lost in what we are saying and we complicate things by saying too much. Saying more is just saying more. It is okay to say very simple and meaningful things. Then let your friend fill in the rest. Do not be afraid of silence.
- Rehearsing your thoughts prior to the dialogue may prove helpful.
- A simple "I am sorry" or "My heart hurts for you" could be sufficient enough to open communication.
- Be prayerful. Ask that you will be sensitive to the gentle whisperings of the Spirit. If you do so, the things you will say will be appropriate and will be heard with open ears and in the intended way.
- Lovingly wrapping your arms around her may be just what she needs.
- Remember your friend needs to hear that you love her and that you care about her.

These relationships with our infertile friends can be developed over a period of time and last endlessly, like mine with Kate or my cousin Anna. Or they can be brief but meaningful encounters such as with my temple friend. Regardless, the power of connection can make an impression on someone's heart and can give her encouragement to continue forward.

Am I saying you should seek out those people who are suspiciously infertile, hunt them down, and make them your projects? No. But I am saying that you should welcome opportunities to reach out to those who cross your path and make an effort to lift their burden for a season. As you speak words of compassion, you can help dry tears of sorrow, heal wounded hearts, and restore hope to the hopeless. Simultaneously, you will begin to identify miracles and blessings interwoven in the lives of your friends, bringing encouragement into your own life. Look for these opportunities and feel that joy!

Preserve Your Marriage

At first glance, the word *preserve* may not conjure up the best images of marriage. Honestly, it makes me think of a dusty jar of peaches floating in a sugary juice and sitting on a shelf in a darkened room. Not exactly a perfect picture of marriage, is it? But to preserve also means to spare, to shield or shelter, to uphold or sustain, "to keep up or to maintain, to keep safe from harm or injury, [or] to protect."[7]

That is a much better picture. How can you keep your marriage safe from the chronic effects of infertility? How can you sustain it through the pangs of disappointments?

For a moment, let's return to our story about Hannah from the Old Testament. At the climax of the biblical account, we know that Hannah became so overcome by her feelings of sorrow such that she wept intensely and decided not to eat. Her husband, Elkanah, with great love and adoration, stepped in and made an intriguing plea, "Hannah, why weepest thou? and why eatest thou not? and why is thy heart grieved? am not I better to thee than ten sons?" (1 Samuel 1:8). I am convinced that he knew very well why she was weeping and why her heart was so grieved, so he really didn't need to ask.

However, to me, Elkanah's plea says that perhaps he was frustrated that Hannah was not seeing, celebrating, or even paying attention to all the good in her life, even the blessing of him, her husband. Maybe Elkanah even felt a bit ignored while Hannah was fretting about her childless status. Perhaps he saw that his efforts to improve the situation weren't making one bit of difference. Wouldn't you love to have seen what else occurred during this tender interchange between husband and wife? Whatever happened during these quiet moments with her husband strengthened Hannah's resolve, so much so that she began to eat and drink, and became determined to go to the temple to pray. Yes, she was still sad. In fact, we read that when she went to the temple, "she was in bitterness of soul," and as she "prayed unto the Lord," she "wept sore" (1 Samuel 1:10). Regardless, Elkanah somehow helped Hannah come to herself, to regain perspective, and to move forward with strength.

We need to be careful that infertility and the quest for conception does not become an obsession that overshadows the marriage relationship. The old biblical counsel of "therefore shall a man leave his father and his mother, and shall cleave unto his wife: and they shall be one flesh," (Genesis 2:24) is still in force. In fact, it is reemphasized in modern revelation as "Thou shalt love thy wife with all thy heart, and shalt cleave unto her and none else" (D&C 42:22). Of course, I do not have to tell you that these scriptures are just as applicable in the reverse: a woman must also leave her father and mother and cleave unto her husband.

President Spencer W. Kimball said, "When the Lord says *all* thy heart, it allows for no sharing nor dividing nor depriving. . . . The words *none else* eliminate everyone and everything. The spouse then becomes preeminent in the life of the husband or wife, and neither social life nor occupational life nor political life nor any other interest nor persons nor things shall ever take precedence over the companion spouse."[8] I think infertility can safely be considered "any other interest."

Infertility can be destructive to a marriage relationship. Differences in opinion may arise as you make decisions—you will inevitably be faced with significant moral and eternal dilemmas. Obsession with becoming pregnant can easily skew your priorities. Chronic stress produced by procedures and the financial burden can open the door to a myriad of destructive elements. All of these things can cause a destroying influence to disrupt your marriage.

Are you and your spouse walking side by side on the same path, holding hands, or are you on a wide road separated by a median and walking in two different directions? Sometimes infertility causes couples to feel as though they have been transported to a place they do not understand and have no way of interpreting. They begin to feel inadequate and unable to conquer it or to move beyond it.[9]

Having a plan for infertility can be helpful in focusing your energies and attention. This plan could include these questions:

- How long will you attempt to conceive without any medical intervention?

- When will you discuss infertility with your doctor?
- When will you consider consulting a reproductive endocrinologist or other fertility specialist?
- How do you both feel about the various types of infertility treatments; for example, medications, surgery, artificial insemination, IVF, and so on?
- How many times will you try each treatment?
- How much money are you willing to spend on treatments; both a total and annual amount (you should also learn how much your health insurance will cover)?
- How will you pay for treatments not covered by insurance?
- If a certain treatment fails, how will you decide whether to try another cycle, move on to a different type of treatment, or quit completely?
- Will you consider adoption?
- Will you ever consider counseling or support to help you cope with the stresses of infertility and at what point you would seek this support?[10]

Once you have established your plan, be in agreement and stay in agreement. Additionally, you should evaluate your plan regularly. Aside from your plan, make sure you protect your marriage by going on dates, setting some goals unrelated to baby-making, learning what your spouse needs from you and providing it, and being sensitive to the emotions of your spouse. Establish "time-outs," when you keep yourself away from anything associated with infertility. When all is said and done, when a treatment is successful or unsuccessful, who do you have? You have each other. Do not sacrifice your marriage for infertility and do not let it become compromised. I believe that if you can preserve a good relationship with your spouse, you will endure this trial. It is not a disease that affects only one of you. It affects you both.

Now, I have one last thing to emphasize about preserving your marriage. In moments of frustration, it is easy to share our sad feelings with a best friend, a sibling, or a parent. As women, we have a tendency to rely on Mom or a girl friend because we feel that other women can better understand our emotions and it is often easier to communicate those emotions to them. For men, it might be easier to keep those feelings bottled up, hoping they will go away. But who should be the first person in your life that you go to for strength? Who should you share those bottled up feelings with? Am I saying that you should not share your sad feelings with a friend or parents? No. What I am saying is that you should not set your spouse aside and go straight to friends and family for convenient support.

Additionally, trust your spouse enough to share those difficult and overwhelming feelings. Yes, there will be a learning curve, a period of time that you will probably have to make a concerted effort to explain your feelings, but it is absolutely essential to communicate with your spouse. It is also important to listen carefully, to be supportive, to be understanding, and to be loving, so that you can establish a feeling of trust as you share this trial. Also, remember some things need to stay between husband and wife. A spouse's responsibility to support, strengthen, and to counsel with the other should never be replaced by anyone else.

President Spencer W. Kimball's counseled, "Frequently, people continue to cleave unto their mothers and their fathers and their [friends]. Sometimes mothers will not relinquish the hold they have had upon their children, and husbands as well as wives return to their mothers and fathers to obtain advice and counsel and to confide, whereas cleaving should be to the wife in most things, and all intimacies should be kept in great secrecy and privacy from others."[11]

Neither husband nor wife should feel that they are uninvolved in decisions, conversations, or the emotions pertaining to infertility. Neither should feel that someone else has taken their place in the relationship. Even though it is often so difficult to share feelings and concerns, it must be done. Perhaps part of the test is learning to communicate with each other, learning to share feelings, and learning to understand the feelings of the other. Perhaps part of the test is learning to rely on each other in *all* things.

I remember specific times when I was so overcome with sadness and disappointment that all I wanted was to have my husband be just as sad as I was. I wanted him to cry. I wanted him to be upset at each failure. But he was not. Perhaps that made me even more upset. All of the words in the world could not even help him understand what it was like for me, a woman, to be denied something that is part of what I know is eternally important for me. Conversely, all of the words in the world could not help me understand his perspective. There was one time when I asked him why he did not cry about our infertility. He simply explained that with each month's disappointment, he didn't find reason to become immobilized. To him, he thought next month was another good time to look for success. How optimistic! When twenty-eight days ticks away without success, optimism is often hard to come by for me.

Marriage is a wonderful part of the plan of Heavenly Father! I can see His great love for us in setting this as the divine design of eternity. As we learn to be companions in this earth life, preserving our marriage through all the challenges and trials we face, we will be able to be together forever. What a great reward. But what a great blessing here and now! If we work together, we have someone we can love, respect, rely on, trust, and receive great strength from. How grateful I am for my marriage and the gift that it is as both of us learn from the trial of infertility.

Notes

1. Cooper-Hilbert, *Infertility and Involuntary Childlessness*, 74.
2. Sheri Dew, "Are We Not All Mothers?" *Ensign*, Nov. 2001, 97.
3. Russel M. Nelson, "Lessons from Eve," *Ensign*, Nov. 1987, 87–88.
4. "Dealing With Infertility and Childlessness," http://www.foreverfamilies.net/xml/articles/childless_couples.aspx?&publication=short.
5. Cooper-Hilbert, *Infertility and Involuntary Childlessness*, 74.
6. Naomi Judd, interview by Jane Pauley, *The Jane Pauley Show*, NBC, Season 1, episode 17, first aired September 21, 2004.
7. "Preserve," Dictionary.com, *The American Heritage Dictionary of the English Language*, fourth edition, Houghton Mifflin Company, 2004, http://dictionary.reference.com/browse/preserve.
8. Spencer W. Kimball, *Faith Precedes the Miracle* (Salt Lake City: Deseret Book, 1972), 142–43.
9. See Beth Cooper-Hilbert, *Infertility and Involuntary Childlessness*, 57.
10. See "My Fertility Planning Guide," Fertility LifeLines, http://www.fertilitylifelines.com/assets/pdfs/fertilitylifelinesresources/myfertilityplan_guide.pdf.
11. Spencer W. Kimball, "Oneness in Marriage," *Ensign*, Mar. 1977, 5.

CHAPTER THIRTEEN

A New Song

Not long ago, I was stung by a bee. It has probably been decades since my last bee sting, but I am positive this one was abnormally painful. Somehow this angry insect found the thin layer of skin on my right temple (on my head) and decided to sting me there. I cannot begin to describe how excruciating the pain was—the pain was so intense that I lost the ability to think straight. I began sweating profusely, my entire head ached, and all I really wanted to do was cry. My mother was with me and acted quickly by pulling the stinger out. Luckily, I found some bee sting ointment, and amazingly enough, it acted rather quickly, taking the edge off the pain. It never removed the pain entirely, but I was indeed grateful that it worked wonders in reducing the intensity so I could return to normal functioning, stop sweating, and regain control.

I can find many lessons from this experience, but the one I find most profound is the power of a balm. A balm is something that soothes or alleviates a pain. Undoubtedly, each of us have had occasion to use a balm of some sort during our lives, so all of us have experienced the relief that it can bring. How grateful I was on that day to find a balm that could be applied to the intense pain caused by such a tiny creature. It was amazing how quickly the balm soothed the pain so I no longer was overwhelmed and immobilized by something that hurt so badly.

We all know that the pain of infertility can be immobilizing—yes, even so overwhelming that we cannot think straight. Sometimes all we want to do is cry. Other times we can't even decide how to feel. Each one of the ideas I have suggested in the past few chapters has the potential of being a balm that can soothe a painful wound. The sting or hurt may never go away entirely, which is normal, but we can reduce the pain to the point that it does not overwhelm us or cause us to be unproductive.

I hope your minds have been opened to some possible ways to cope during this trial. Some of my ideas might seem far from helpful to you personally, while some seem easy enough to try tomorrow. You may have laughed about a few or thought I was crazy in suggesting others. Regardless, I hope that you will at least consider them. Instead of dismissing them, try them; put them to the test. Perhaps you and your spouse can decide together which ones to try now and which to save for later. Ultimately, I want to show that there *are* ways you can cope. Find what works best for you. Adapt what I have said to fit your circumstance. Add other ideas as they come to you, as my list is far from complete.

There is no guarantee that any of the strategies I have come up with will solve your problem or remove the entirety of your sorrow, but I promise you that each of them have the healing properties of a balm: they can alleviate the sting and provide a way for you to enjoy life despite the sorrow.

I also realize that some of you may be suffering deeper wounds that cannot be remedied by these suggestions. Chronic strain and crisis can cause pains that may only be relieved only through professional help. In fact, serious psychological disorders can develop as a result of infertility. For you, I plead with you to seek help! Bishops are wonderful. They are blessed with a great mantle of discernment, love, and compassion. They can recommend counselors through LDS Family Services who will share your moral and religious understanding. OB/GYNs and reproductive endocrinologists can also recommend additional resources for helping couples cope with infertility. It is okay to seek the help of others. I have seen the overwhelming difference made in the life of someone I love when she sought professional counseling. I hope that you can experience happiness and light in your life again.

I know there are days when all seems dark and foreboding, so dark that making an effort to do anything to help better your situation might feel impossible. You might even feel that you would much rather wallow in the misery of it all, simply because it is easier or maybe it feels good to be miserable. Trust me, this is not a place you want to be.

President Dieter F. Uchtdorf counseled,

> The adversary uses despair to bind hearts and minds in suffocating darkness. Despair drains from us all that is vibrant and joyful and leaves behind the empty remnants of what life was meant to be. Despair kills ambition, advances sickness, pollutes the soul, and deadens the heart. Despair can seem like a staircase that leads only and forever downward.
>
> Hope, on the other hand, is like the beam of sunlight rising up and above the horizon of our present circumstances. It pierces the darkness with a brilliant dawn. It encourages and inspires us to place our trust in the loving care of an eternal Heavenly Father, who has prepared a way for those who seek for eternal truth in a world of relativism, confusion, and of fear. . . .
>
> . . . To all who suffer—to all who feel discouraged, worried, or lonely—I say with love and deep concern for you, never give in. Never surrender. Never allow despair to overcome your spirit. Embrace and rely upon the Hope of Israel, for the love of the Son of God pierces all darkness, softens all sorrow, and gladdens every heart.[1]

Christ does not want us to miserable. He wants us to be happy and full of hope. He knows that the experiences of mortality will challenge us even to the depths of sadness, but happiness, even in times of great trial can be ours because of Him. When we feel miserable and feel that all we can see is darkness and confusion, let's commit to ourselves to finding a way to see light and happiness again; let us run to the Savior and seek His infinite help.

The Lord offers us the greatest healing balm possible. Through His Atonement, He suffered so that our suffering would not be more than we could bear. In Doctrine and Covenants 19, Christ revealed to Joseph Smith how intensely painful His suffering in Gethsemane was. Additionally, Christ explained the eternal reasoning behind his suffering: "I, God, have suffered these things for all, that they might not suffer if they would repent" (v. 16). Elder Jeffrey R. Holland clarified Christ's words beautifully, "In our moments of pain and trial, I guess we would shudder to think it could be worse, but the answer to that is clearly that it could be worse and it would be worse. Only through our faith and repentance and obedience to the gospel that provided the sacred Atonement is it kept from being worse."[2]

As you find a way to cope and allow your burden to be upon the Lord, your countenance will change. The way you see yourself, your circumstance, and your trial will be different. The words in Psalm 40 describe this transformation perfectly by comparing it to singing a new song, a song of beauty rather than a song of sadness, bitterness, and misery:

> I waited patiently for the Lord; and he inclined unto me, and heard my cry.
>
> He brought me up also out of an horrible pit, out of the miry clay, and set my feet upon a rock, and established my goings.
>
> And he hath put a new song in my mouth, even praise unto our God: many shall see it . . . and shall trust in the Lord.
>
> Blessed is that man that maketh the Lord his trust...
>
> I delight to do thy will, O my God: yea, thy law is within my heart . . .
>
> Withhold not thou thy tender mercies from me, O Lord: let thy loving kindness and thy truth continually preserve me...
>
> Be pleased, O Lord, to deliver me: O Lord, make haste to help me . . .
>
> But I am poor and needy; yet the Lord thinketh upon me: thou art my help and my deliverer; make no tarrying, O my God. (Psalm 40:1–4, 8, 11, 13, 17)

What song are you singing? What can you do to transform that song into one of greater joy and trust in the Lord?

Notes

1. Dieter F. Uchtdorf, "The Infinite Power of Hope," *Ensign*, Nov. 2008, 22, 24.
2. Jeffrey R. Holland, "Lessons from Liberty Jail," CES Fireside for Young Adults, Sept. 2008.

Part Three

Considering Male Infertility

CHAPTER FOURTEEN

—◈◈◈—

It's Him, Not Me

T his chapter is different than all of the rest simply because I did not write it. I feel, however, that it is crucial that it be included in this book. Not long ago, I was talking with my sister, who is also dealing with infertility. She told me about a dear friend of hers who was part of her network, a friend who was dealing with infertility. As my sister described her friend's situation, I was intrigued and felt certain that her story needed to be told. Her story reaches out to the audience that I cannot fully reach: couples who experience male factor infertility solely. When I asked her to tell her story, I gave her a list of questions to consider and requested her to answer in written form. When I received her responses, the document was twenty pages in 12 point Times New Roman font! She certainly went above and beyond my expectations. Her responses are truly valuable and I could never retell them and do so effectively; therefore, I have included her exact narrative. To her, I say thank you, although it does not adequately describe the gift she has given. As I give it to you, I hope that it will give you greater perspective. And, more specifically, to those whose lives are described by her, I hope that it provides you with words that speak peace to your heart and gives some voice to your struggle.

Matt and Leslie

Matt and I have known each other since our junior year of high school. We met through some mutual friends, dated, went our separate ways for college, and got back together after Matt's mission. After my junior year of college, we were married and thought we would wait a little bit to start our family—not too long, however, just long enough to adjust to being married. My sister had gotten married a few months before us and when her little girl was born a year after we were married, we looked at that sweet little girl and decided that we were ready. Little did we know what awaited us and just how much more preparation Heavenly Father had in store.

Once we had been married for about three years, trying to conceive for two, we decided to get serious with medical intervention. Those first few years were truly agonizing. Surrounded by neighbors and friends having child after child, we spent month after month imagining up pregnancy symptoms and counting the number of days until I could take one of the early response pregnancy tests. When test after test after test came back negative (not even a hint of that double stripe), we were sure that we needed some medical help. I started doing blood tests to check my hormone levels, ducking out to my car during work to make appointments or discuss the results. The results pointed to my body being just fine.

Our doctor recommended that Matt undergo a semen analysis. This was not welcome news to him, but we got the name of the lab, went to our appointment, and then waited for results. When I received a call from the office about the semen analysis, I was told that Matt's semen quality was poor . . . he had both low motility and odd morphology. I had to take a few minutes to recover before I went back to work. The doctor wanted us to complete another analysis to verify the results since "everyone has a bad day every now and then." I carried the burden of the news with me for the rest of the day and later that night I had the unfortunate task of giving Matt the results. He was immediately frustrated and was determined that our next attempt would yield better results. Because of complications with collecting semen samples, however, further results ended up not coming for three years.

During these years, while Matt felt disheartened, demoralized, and humiliated, I spent a lot of time feeling frustrated and completely helpless. Most days I just wished that I was the one with the medical issue so I could take care of it, and we could get on with our family. When

I would bring up the subject of making appointments and consulting the doctor, I often felt like I was putting unwelcome pressure on him. While I felt as though we did not talk to each other very much about our infertility, Matt felt like it was *all* that we talked about. I spent months trying to be patient, not bringing it up, and waiting for him to take the initiative.

I felt like I needed to do something, but the only thing I could do was continue to ascertain the status of my reproductive system; I was embarrassingly unfamiliar with its processes, so I began to be more pro-active and assertive in my treatment. During this time, we relocated to Texas and eventually we contacted a fertility center to begin treatment. I always consult books when I have questions or struggles, and I have read many books on infertility. One of the things I found in my reading was that the husband is often behind the wife, by at least a year, in terms of enthusiasm for pursuing fertility treatment. This difference proved especially true in our situation. While Matt and I were at different places on our scale of enthusiasm, over time, it has been most rewarding to see a change come about in Matt and to see him become more enthusiastic about our options.

An added benefit to my reading was the sense of empowerment that I felt about our situation. As I became more knowledgeable about my body, Matt's body, and possible treatment options, I could better advocate for us in the medical setting.

One of the main mistakes I made during our struggle, however, was not acknowledging my own feelings about infertility. Matt, on the other hand, has been good at identifying his feelings. He doesn't verbalize them very much, but he acknowledges that this trial has affected him deeply. I am a positive and happy person by nature, and I determined that I was not going to be the stereotypical infertility patient who is bitter and doesn't like baby showers and doesn't like hearing that friends are pregnant. I told myself that I needed to be happy for everyone who could get pregnant. I think I made it harder on us because I tried to put a positive spin on *everything*. In a lot of ways, I think the way I talked about our infertility affected Matt's willingness to open up and share his feelings. Now that we are both admitting the reality of our feelings, we are more comfortable talking about it with each other. I do not try to convince him to see the silver lining, and he patiently endures my ramblings and various "what if" scenarios.

At our first visit to the fertility center in Texas, we underwent a consultation with a reproductive endocrinologist. After a review of our previous tests and an ultrasound, the doctor told us that everything he saw pointed to male factor infertility and that his first recommendation was to pursue IVF. In order to confirm his diagnosis, he requested that we collect another semen sample, preferably right there, that day in their lab. However, with another failed attempt, we left the center. Any prospect of pursuing further treatments seemed bleak if we couldn't even collect semen.

Words cannot describe how horrible it felt to me, and so I certainly cannot begin to imagine what it was like for Matt. I desperately wanted him to come through this with little emotional damage but, the longer it went on, the worse it seemed to get. I often felt stuck in a difficult situation because I knew he felt horrible about it, and I didn't want to bring it up. In the meantime, I also felt frustrated because we went back to testing me for other things. I was trying so hard to find something wrong with me, but all the evidence pointed to him. I was being poked, prodded, and subjected to all kinds of tests when that wasn't the most productive path. The clearest path was the one that we just couldn't seem to take. My journal records:

> I have to keep going to the doctor. I have to take vitamins and pills every day. I have to take my temperature, I have to have these tests done and his only request is that we not talk about it. Well, I need to talk about it! I do at least five things a day that point straight at it—it's in front of my face all the time and I don't feel like we're in it together. I feel like he's just waiting for me to figure out what's wrong with me so we can have kids. In the meantime he's going to pretend like there's nothing wrong. I need more patience . . . much more patience.

I think this quote from my journal describes my feelings over the several years that we waited to have our male factor diagnosis confirmed. I went back and forth a lot between having compassion for Matt and the struggle that it is for him and feeling the struggle myself. Looking back, I wish I had done a better job of supporting him, but since our approaches to the problem were completely different, we weren't communicating well.

Matt admits that he is even angrier now than when we started out. From his comments, I think a lot of this anger is linked to the fact that the problem originates with his body. I have never considered our infertility as his problem; it is our problem. *We* have male factor infertility. We have trouble getting our eggs and sperm together at the right time. I know that because his body is not cooperating affects him more than I realize. I have learned that he has to deal with it in his own way. Sometimes I wish I understood "his way" better, but I know I need to be patient and respect him because that is the same generosity he affords me. As we have been able to be more open with each other, we have cleared some misunderstandings and miscommunications. Of course, we do have more work to do in this area.

Even though we were consciously trying to stay close, many times I felt our divergent coping paths were going to lead us so far apart that I wasn't sure we would make it back together again emotionally. The times when we did talk about our infertility seemed to make me feel even worse because my perspective (seeing the good in life, recognizing how we can be blessed through our trials) was maddening to him, and his perspective (anger, bitterness, pessimism) was maddening to me. All the while, I had a hard time believing that those negative emotions were his "best effort."

It has also been difficult to see that our experience with infertility has affected our spirituality so differently—I have felt strengthened in my faith while he says his has been unaffected. His comments suggest that faith is even harder for him to come by these days. There are so many journal entries where I mention that I wanted to "scream" or where I "just cried and cried" because of the trial itself and his seeming malaise. At the same time, I appreciated the good things that he was doing and recognized that infertility is a small part of our relationship— we love each other for a lot of reasons. Even though having a family is one of those key reasons, there is a lot we can appreciate about being together even if we don't have children.

It has been helpful to me to recognize how pride has affected my perspective and reactions. Despite the fact that we both were exercising pride to some extent, I had to come to terms with a great reality of life: I can only control *my* emotions and reactions. This fact is one way I have moved on, compartmentalized the problem, and worked to keep our marriage strong. Although it was difficult, I finally learned that I had to believe Matt, to trust that he really was working through his emotions, and respect it as his way of coping. I have certainly learned a great deal about patience and longsuffering, perhaps more than I would have any other way.

There have been many times when I prayed for guidance and direction, and most of the time the prayer was "please help us to have children." It took almost five years for me to learn to pray differently. All along, I have looked at infertility as a big problem instead of as individual issues to resolve. It took desperately needing a semen analysis for me to pray for help accomplishing that specific task. It seemed to be an interesting thing to pray for, but I prayed my heart out for it and for our bodies to manifest our problems and obstacles to conception. I had always heard people who spoke of asking to know what they should pray for and I never really understood it until then. Once I was completely broken and humble, without any idea what to do, I was willing to go to Heavenly Father and say, "What should I ask for now?" This new way of praying not only helped us reach crucial fertility benchmarks, it also taught me to appreciate those benchmarks.

I have never been as relieved and grateful as when we collected that second semen sample successfully. It had been over three years since our first attempt and almost two years since our last attempt, and blessedly, we could move forward. Did we have children yet? No. Did we have a course of action yet? No. But we did take a huge step toward accomplishing our goal. From my journal, it was apparent that things were starting to look up:

> A miracle has happened in our house. Yesterday, Matt called to tell me that Dr. Perry (a urologist he met through a work event) had called him to talk about his semen analysis. Dr. Perry told him it was low and made an appointment for him for the following week. Last night Matt just kept talking about it and the ramifications. He said 'Maybe that is the problem—since they haven't found anything wrong with you yet right?' I about fell off my chair. . . . Those words out of Matt's mouth were a miracle because up until now he's not been willing to admit that there are any problems with [him]. I'm amazed and humbled.

Matt making the contact and starting a dialogue with the urologist said a lot about Matt's level of commitment to pursuing fertility treatments. It became an even greater blessing since Matt would later need to have his varicocele (a jumble of tangled blood vessels around the spermatic cord that impair sperm production in large measure due to the amount of heat that they generate) operated on, and we felt comfortable and confident with this urologist. I felt extreme gratitude. At that point, we still had a lot to learn and quite a few hurdles to jump, but we were slowly starting to see blessings because of our faith and constant prayers. I could not be more grateful for Heavenly Father's generous hand in our lives.

Matt went to an appointment with the urologist by himself and when I did not hear from him that day, I figured the news was not good. I really wasn't ready to hear it until a few hours after he got home. Up to that point, I had understood that we would need to get the varicocele fixed, and then we would be on our way to fertility. After talking with the urologist, we came to understand the problem differently. Our previous doctor had not discussed with us the nature of varicoceles: the longer they go untreated the worse the damage they can do and that damage is irreparable. The urologist said that through surgery, which he recommended, he could stop the problem from getting worse but it was impossible for him to give back the 19 million sperm that we had lost over the past three years. Even after the surgery, the doctor thought that IVF would be our only option for conceiving.

This news was a huge disappointment for both of us. We now had to come to terms with Matt having a major surgery and even after that, the likelihood that the only way our children could be conceived was in a petri dish in a lab somewhere. This is from my journal on that day:

> You know, I haven't asked the question "Why me?" in a long time but my heart begs the question again. As I think about it I wonder if it's because Heavenly Father knows . . . this is something we want so badly that we'll do whatever we can for it. The prospect is not a thrilling one, but it's comforting to remember that the Lord will not send more than we can handle and that Matt and I have been blessed and will continue to be blessed by this trial as we do all things that lie in our power and to stand still and be assured that the Lord will manifest His arm.

We determined that surgery was the best option. I had been reading and researching IVF, and I was slowly accepting the prospect of it, but it was still overwhelming. This urologist put us in contact with a brand new fertility center that was being built not ten minutes from our house! I made an appointment, and Matt and I met with the doctor for the first time.

I had started to feel my biological clock ticking, and so before our appointment we started to consider doing IVF now and then doing the surgery after I was pregnant. That way we didn't have to "waste" the year it would take for the results of the surgery to show. I wanted babies, I had waited long enough, and I wanted them now! After tearfully discussing our situation and looking at our options with the doctor, he actually recommended that we pursue the surgery first to see what improvements could be made naturally.

He recognized that I was emotionally at the end of my rope and suggested that I consider speaking with a counselor. The doctor needed my emotional credit card to be at zero because it would be maxed out with IVF. He recommended a local psychologist who had experience in helping people with fertility issues. He encouraged us to go home, think about our options, and make a decision. He emphasized that "whatever we chose would be the right choice." I loved this office already. He took the time to answer questions and even suggested that we explore all avenues before we committed to any assisted reproductive technology. We appreciated that he did not pressure us into a particular path.

As I gave our situation some good solid thought and as Matt and I talked about it, we realized that my selfish motives were not a good reason for determining a course of action. We had finally arrived at a place where we could do something to resolve the problem, and I just wanted to do it, but I had to realize that even with the information, we still needed to work on the Lord's timeline. Matt was, as always, level-headed and able to look at the situation from a more objective point of view. He valued my opinion while also keeping us focused on solid facts. At this point, I also started to realize how much this challenge of infertility had affected me mentally and emotionally.

I spoke with the counselor that our doctor had recommended, and I was immediately glad that I had done so. I wish I had gone years earlier!

After spending a few months with a professional counselor, trying to determine all the ways that I was not letting this struggle get to me, I came to realize that infertility represents loss on many different levels: we lost our naïveté, we lost our ideal family setup, we lost some romance and intimacy, and, in a lot of ways, we lost our innocence. A process that occurs so naturally for so many is not available to us, and I learned that it was important to recognize the effect of that fact. In President Faust's talk "The Healing Power of Forgiveness" in the May 2007 *Ensign*, he talks about humbly acknowledging less-than-charitable feelings and asking for help to deal with them. So now, instead of covering up those feelings and pretending that I do not have them, the more constructive thing to do is reason them out or realize that those feelings and frustrations make up a small part of who I am and they don't define everything.

Because of her experience with infertility patients, my counselor had other cases to draw from in terms of what was "normal," and I was actually surprised to find out how normal my feelings were. Gradually, I started to feel like myself again instead of a fertility-obsessed wife. Initially, Matt was far from comfortable with the idea of me going to counseling, but I insisted that it would help me and, in turn, us. He was concerned about what I would talk about. I explained that the counselor was helping me figure some things out. I explained that it was as though we were dumping the contents of my brain on the table and then trying to fit the pieces together. It was hard to go without his support, but it turned out to be such a good thing that he recognized the results before too long. I smile today when I hear him say, "Leslie went to counseling and it really helped her," as he encourages someone else to go or as he defends someone's decision to begin counseling. I think he had to realize that I wasn't going because there was something wrong with me or us, but that I was going because I wanted to be the best person I could and at the time, I was struggling to do that on my own.

Initially, I was hesitant to go to counseling because I had been relying on the Savior and I knew that He could heal anything. During this time, I came to the conclusion that, yes, He could heal anything, but I needed to give Him my best efforts and employ all the tools possible in order for Him to help me feel whole. I found that counseling coupled with the Spirit, in addition to daily prayer and scripture study, went a long way to helping me feel like myself again. I was actually pleasantly surprised at some of the things I realized as a result. I started to see strengths that Matt and I had that I failed to see before. I began to realize that during this difficult season, my faith was growing into knowledge. I was emerging with my newfound self, and I liked what I was seeing.

During that summer, we moved forward with our plans for surgery. We were both apprehensive, but Matt was definitely the most nervous. Though side effects are rare and science has the procedure of varicocelectomy down to an art, there was that small chance that something could happen to a crucial part of him. As I watched his nervousness, I stood back in appreciation for his willingness to work so hard for us to have a family. The four previous years had been increasingly difficult with many tears and frustrations, but we were finally both in tune with each other, and that faded the memory of many of those feelings. As the surgery drew closer, we shared details with our families, and Matt asked for a blessing from some close friends. From my perspective, this request for a blessing seemed to be a Herculean task for him. As our friends came over, they were rather shocked to find out about his surgery and what it entailed (because we hadn't been talking about it to anyone). I was so proud of Matt as he explained what was going to happen and why it needed to happen. During this phase and after, I have recognized the deep humility and faith that he has and is continuing to develop.

Matt was stoic during the pre-op and surgery. True to his great personality, when he decides on a course of action, he is duty-bound to see it through. He calmed my nerves as we waited for the surgical team to arrive. After the surgery, the doctor told us it had gone well and that he had found what he expected and did what he expected to do. Those words were comforting. Knowing that sperm take three months to develop and knowing that his body would need some recovery time before sperm production could be back to his new "normal," our urologist scheduled a follow-up appointment for six months out.

It was interesting how the mood in our marriage shifted after the surgery. I felt like a weight had been lifted from my shoulders, but I think Matt felt like one had been put on his. As he continued to recover, he became more open about our situation and spoke more candidly with friends and family. I don't know how hard this was for him, but I appreciated the growing support we were receiving.

At our six-month follow-up, we were both hoping for a miracle. We were hoping that his testosterone and sperm levels were normal. We were happy to find out that doses of Clomid were helping with his hormone levels, but we were devastated to find that the semen analysis had not changed. We were seeing the results that had been promised, but we had been hoping for something more. At this point, we were left to decide whether to pursue IVF or work toward adoption. We, of course, pondered both options very seriously, and we are on track for IVF this summer. As we have made a conscious effort to prepare for the procedure this summer, we have—well, mostly I—have spent a lot of time reflecting on our journey thus far, and the things we have learned and been through. Last summer, I felt like a year was such a long time, especially since we would just be waiting. However, I have found so many sweet moments as I have thought back through the lessons Heavenly Father has taught me. I feel like this last year has been a blessing—a time of rejoicing—when I have been able to introspectively commune with heaven about the past and humbly seek help for the future.

As I reflect on the past several years, I recall times when I'd get so discouraged and hopeless. During those time, I was keenly reminded of the Savior's hand in my life. Even though I could not fathom why He would want us to endure such a horrible, demoralizing experience, I would try to muster up a bit more faith to make it through. My faith was strengthened as I relied heavily on the scriptures, my relationship with the Holy Ghost, my opportunities to serve, the power of prayer, my perspective of endurance, and relationships with others.

Scriptures

Over the past five years I have used the scriptures as a lifeline. I have learned some powerful lessons as I have depended on the scriptures to show me what Heavenly Father would teach me. Initially, I committed to studying the scriptures so I could quickly learn what I needed to get on with this trial. Eventually it turned into a time of communion, and many truths began to be opened to me. I learned how to listen to the

Spirit and applied the lessons of the gospel to my own life. My experience has been sweet as I have followed the counsel of Nephi to liken all scriptures unto me because it truly has been for my profit and learning.

I love Isaiah! Isaiah 61:3 has been especially applicable to my life: "To appoint unto them that mourn in Zion, to give unto them beauty for ashes, the oil of joy for mourning, the garment of praise for the spirit of heaviness; that they might be called trees of righteousness, the planting of the Lord, that he might be glorified." At times it is hard to believe that I will receive the promise of beauty and joy, or that I will glorify the Lord by remaining righteousness in my struggle. But then I see glimpses, sometimes very small glimpses, that Heavenly Father will keep His promise.

Recently, I have been blessed with insight and understanding beyond what I ever expected, and I see this promise fulfilled. I have learned that because He is the redeeming Savior, Christ has the power to turn our greatest sorrow into our greatest joy, even before the promise of children is fulfilled. I have also learned, however, that in order to feel the joy promised by the Savior, we must delve into the depths of sorrow; we have to know pain and suffering so that He can teach us joy. Over these difficult years, I feel as though my sorrow has increased greatly, but at the other end of the spectrum, my potential for joy has also grown immensely.

Relationship with the Holy Ghost

The Holy Ghost has been crucial to my well-being and has strengthened my faith. I have a testimony that the Holy Ghost does indeed bring things to our remembrance, and just when we need them. It is, of course, critical that we put things in our minds for Him to remind us of; after all, He must have something to work with. On one particularly tough day several years ago, I went to the temple. I was spent. I didn't feel like I had much left in my faith reservoir, and I wanted to know when our prayers would be answered. I had the distinct thought, "I still have more to teach you." This thought related so beautifully to a section in my patriarchal blessing. At that moment, I realized that the Holy Ghost helped bring this sweet assurance to my remembrance, and it gave me great comfort and peace. I sat in the temple and simply reflected on the joy and gratitude that I felt from heaven. Time and again, small bits of inspiration like this came and washed away the frustration I felt while waiting for another answer or for guidance with a decision. My question was not always answered and my problem was far from solved, but I had another example of the Lord's knowledge of me and my individual needs. I knew that He loved me, that He knew me, and I was confident that He was directing my life. Those experiences, in what were some of my darkest hours, have led me to a firm testimony of the reality of His existence and a sure knowledge of the Father, the Son, and the Comforter. How grateful I am for the strength, comfort, and love I derive from a close relationship with Them!

It is interesting to me to observe how cyclical our relationship with Deity is, in any phase of life. Just when you think Heaven isn't listening, and you start to stumble in the dark, you find just enough light to move ahead with confidence. It has been and will always be a blessing in my life to go back to the Savior for understanding and guidance.

Opportunities to Serve

Service to others has helped increase the Spirit in my life while also giving me an increased capacity to love and understand others. One of my favorite scripture passages is 2 Corinthians 1:3–7:

> Blessed be God, even the Father of our Lord Jesus Christ, the Father of mercies, and the God of all comfort;
>
> Who comforteth us in all our tribulation, that we may be able to comfort them which are in any trouble, by the comfort wherewith we ourselves are comforted of God.
>
> For as the sufferings of Christ abound in us, so our consolation also aboundeth by Christ.
>
> And whether we be afflicted, it is for your consolation and salvation, which is effectual in the enduring of the same sufferings which we also suffer: or whether we be comforted, it is for your consolation and salvation.
>
> And our hope of you is stedfast, knowing, that as ye are partakers of the sufferings, so shall ye be also of the consolation.

I know that as I have reached out to others, no matter what their struggles in life, the Lord has indeed blessed me with comfort and consolation, for both myself and for those I am serving. This comfort was especially crucial during the years when the Savior was my only support; when I had to rely on Him alone, He did not disappoint. Evidence of His love and His awareness of me abounded in so many areas of my life.

I could see that He knew me and was guiding my life as I was given the opportunity to be a visiting teacher to some sisters who were having some especially hard challenges. At times, their challenges heaping upon my own was particularly overwhelming, but as I remembered the promise in 2 Corinthians, I willingly gave Christ the burden and found comfort. It was amazing to see how the Savior blessed me with clear insight and pure inspiration. Through many experiences with service, but especially in visiting teaching, I know that He was directing my efforts, which meant that He knew me. Over and over, He inspired me to be in the right place at the right time or to do the right thing for one of these sweet sisters.

I realized through this experience, and others like it, that the Lord is mindful of all of us. And on the days that I didn't feel like He was mindful of me, I could recall evidence that He was. If He had used me to help someone else, He knew her and He knew me. As I drew closer to Him, He drew closer to me, and I found that I began to know more about Him.

The Power of Prayer

I am grateful the blessing of speaking to Heavenly Father about my struggles and greatest desires. Even though I know that He is always there, there have been times when I felt a strong desire to talk about my feelings with my family or close friends. Because of the nature of our problem, however, Matt preferred that we not disclose information to our family members. This was especially difficult, as our families would ask questions about our situation. They knew that we wanted to have children, and they knew that we were pursuing tests and other treatment options, but we simply gave them vague half-answers while trying to bring the conversation to a quick close. So much of me wanted to explode with the disappointment and frustration, but out of respect for Matt and the personal nature of our struggle, I knew that I needed to keep quiet. As time went on, I realized that this situation drew me much closer to my Heavenly Father. As I poured out my soul to Him in fervent prayer, I received answers and strength. I was still frustrated that I couldn't talk with close friends, but this helped me to learn to think twice before disclosing private information.

Perspective on Endurance

Learning more about endurance has also strengthened my faith. Of course, I look forward to the day when this trial will be behind us, but due to the length of time we have experienced it, I have learned about enduring patiently. It is one thing to keep the faith when you can see the light at the end of the tunnel, but it is something entirely different to patiently endure, while faithfully waiting for the Lord's will to become evident. This excerpt from my journal is during the sixth year of my enduring:

> I used to be a little hesitant to recite this line of the 13th Article of Faith—"we hope to be able to endure all things." Who of us would sign up to endure all things? It has only been recently that I have come to better understand this scripture and a small part of the effort involved in learning endurance.
>
> When I run, I take various routes. One of my favorite paths also happens to be the hardest. Though it's only three miles long, there are several steep hills that always leave me breathless by the time I crest them. In fact, on the days when I take this route I find myself fighting an internal struggle between stopping and just continuing to put one foot in front of the other. It's usually on the way back, when I'm working my way up the last two hills and my lungs are on fire and my muscles are screaming for mercy that I have to put my head down and look ahead just a few steps because to look any further is overwhelming.
>
> It's during those times when I'm having to muster up all traces of resolve left in me that I usually think about endurance. I have to remind myself that I will only learn to run harder, faster, and longer by running courses that are challenging. I tell myself that it is the effort of moving in the midst of pain, obstacle, or weakness that little by little builds my endurance and teaches me how to keep running no matter what. Each step I take on the way up the hill lends me momentum, and even though I've run this way many times, when I make it to the top I'm always surprised at how far I've been able to come. And after my

run, when I get home, the part that I remember most isn't the ease with which I started the run or the relief I felt at its completion, but rather the strength I realized I had when it was hard to keep moving.

I started running about a year after we were married. It is therapeutic for me to put on my running shoes and get out and exercise. Sometimes as I run, I think about endurance, form, progression, and any number of principles that apply to running as well as life in general. During times when I have needed revelation, running has proved an avenue for Heavenly Father to communicate with me.

Relationships with Others

As I have reflected on our journey through infertility, I have realized that there have been times when we have felt left out, socially awkward, frustrated, bitter, angry, and forgotten. Sometimes those feelings made it hard for us to fit in with our peers and other family members. Six years is a long time to feel like the odd man out. At the same time, we have been blessed with family—my mother, grandmothers, aunts, and sisters especially—who have gone the extra mile to pull us in and help us feel valued and appreciated. They have allowed us to smother their children with love and attention and praised us for it; they have been patient with our inexperience and inability to relate on some levels. They have loved us and kept us close during a time when we felt so far from their world, especially during the time when we wouldn't let them into ours. I am so grateful for the strength we have gleaned from their love. During a time when joy can be tough to come by, these opportunities have renewed us and given our lives purpose and meaning.

So far, that is our story. In about a month we will go in for our IVF class. We will learn how to do injections, we will have a mock transfer, and we will review the steps leading up to the transfer. We are hopeful and excited as we take this next step. We look forward to what the future holds for us.

CHAPTER FIFTEEN

---✦✦✦---

That He Might Become the Father of Many Nations

This chapter has been the hardest for me to write. The reason is simple: I am not a man. Because men handle the experiences of life differently from women, I believe that this book needs to include a specific chapter addressing issues men deal with as they face infertility whether it be their own, their wife's, or a combination of both. I have spent hours that could be collected into days and weeks wondering what a man might want to hear. The answers span the spectrum: "There is nothing I need to hear," "How can I fix my wife?" "Teach me how to feel like a man again," and "When can our intimate life get back to normal?" You may be wondering how I, a woman, could even claim to adequately describe a man's struggle with infertility, let alone provide an answer to any of these questions or tell a man how to feel. For that reason, I would like to spend the next several pages exposing your minds to some interesting thoughts and experiences from other men just like you.

This chapter can probably be defined as deficient in many ways, but it is only the beginning of a crucial dialogue that needs to take place. My hope, however, is that it will open the door for conversation to begin and for men to think differently about infertility. As I have approached several men and asked them to share their feelings, I have found that they are reluctant and often closed about the subject. Through this book, and more specifically this chapter, I hope that men will learn that feeling *something* about infertility is a step toward accepting it, and it is even better to share those feelings. It is, of course, not necessary to share those feelings with the world, but a good place to start is with your wife. If a man's ability to name and communicate his feelings to his wife increases or changes such that they can understand each other even a little better, I will feel that I have accomplished something truly magnificent. I know that if we can respectfully communicate our feelings, while striving for unity and understanding, we, as couples, can get closer to healing our wounded hearts and lives.

Learning to See Infertility Through Different Eyes

Historically, infertility has been considered a female problem. Think about it—even in the scriptures, it talks about women who are barren being reproached among men. In some ways, they were considered broken, and because of something beyond their control, they were said to have dishonored their families and, more specifically, their husbands. Wouldn't it be interesting to go back in time and perform the latest tests on these couples to determine what the true cause of a couple's infertility was? I am sure the statistics would have been different then, but I wonder how many cases of infertility were caused by female factor alone.

In our world today, it is estimated that male factor infertility is the sole cause of a couple's infertility in 20 percent of the cases, whereas it is a contributing factor in 30–40 percent of the cases.[1] Male infertility is better diagnosed, better treated, and the prognosis is much better now. Why? Men are beginning to be open to being tested and being a proactive part of treatment. Just think what could be accomplished if we can continue this trend in a positive direction!

As a general rule, when there is a problem conceiving after one year, doctors suggest both husband and wife be tested. It can no longer be assumed that infertility is just a female problem. From day one, it can be most helpful and efficient if both husband and wife are committed to walking the path of infertility together. That means being tested together, talking about infertility together, making decisions together, and even going to appointments together. Dr. James Borin and Natan Bar-Chama encourage us by saying that "for most infertile couples, pregnancy is most efficiently achieved following a comprehensive, coordinated medical approach involving both the male and female. Only by accurately assessing both partners can a physician recommend the most cost-effective, time-efficient, and least emotionally distressing treatments."[2]

It seems many men are reluctant to take part in testing and end up being the last to be analyzed and diagnosed. Perhaps it is because men have a hard time talking about such a sensitive topic or less likely to take care of their health.[3] Perhaps they are afraid that what they find will compromise their masculinity or sexuality, or maybe they fear that "what was formerly private behavior now seems [to become] a very public event."[4] Whatever the reason, we find hope that "there are more men in waiting rooms supporting their spouses through treatments; they are more proactive in seeking information about male factor [infertility] and pursuing therapies."[5]

My perception of how men deal with infertility changed when I finally asked my husband to explain to me how he felt about our infertility. I regret not asking sooner. I must admit that all along, I truly wanted and even expected his reaction to be the same as mine—how naïve is that? I guess I was unrealistically hopeful. I was quite disappointed that he didn't cry every month when I started menstruating, that he didn't think about being infertile every day, and that he didn't seem affected by comments made about the importance of fatherhood at church. I often felt alone and as though having a baby was not a priority to him. My belated conversation with him showed me that I was wrong in being disappointed.

It is important to remind you that male factor infertility was not part of our diagnosis, so our perspective of infertility may be different from a couple who experiences both male and female factor infertility or even from a couple who is challenged with male factor infertility alone.

From Joel's experience and perspective, I learned that infertility was much harder for me than for him. I wonder if it might have anything to do with the fact that from our youth, we are taught about the sacred roles of men and women, which are divinely designed to be different, but compliment each other so perfectly. "The Family: A Proclamation to the World" teaches that "by divine design, fathers are to preside over their families in love and righteousness and are responsible to provide the necessities of life and protection for their families. Mothers are primarily responsible for the nurture of their children."[6] This inspired declaration gives shape to our perspective of life and what we will become. Throughout our lives, we are taught skills that will help us prepare for and be more successful in these roles. If a woman could be a fly on the wall in an Aaronic or Melchizedek Priesthood classroom, she would hear a completely different perspective on life and ways to use gospel principles because of this role difference. The development of these skills is, of course, emphasized in family home evenings, Sunday School lessons, and in the Faith in God, Personal Progress, and Duty to God programs.

So, while "the nurture of their children" becomes a primary focus of women, men must prepare themselves to preside, provide, and protect their families. Having children, therefore, could be seen as a secondary role to a man. It would not be unusual, then, for a woman to feel as though she cannot achieve her divinely appointed role when children do not exist within the family. A man, however, can achieve his primary role regardless of family size. With this perspective, he could easily argue that his job is done once he begins presiding, providing, and protecting his wife. In actuality, however, he must spend the rest of his life perfecting his ability to preside, provide, and protect.

I had never really looked at infertility through these eyes before, have you? With these new eyes, I could see why my husband did not feel as cheated as I did. He admitted that he was more discouraged and frustrated about my emotions and how infertility was affecting me than he was about his own feelings about infertility. When we experienced the monthly setbacks, it took me several days to put it behind me while his response was "Better luck next time" or "Let's try again next month!"

In our tell-all conversation, he did share that his frustrations began to increase when the medical procedures began. The invasive procedures, injections, financial strain, and time commitment affected his emotions because they had become more tangible to him. Previously, the monthly periods were just an indirect and secondhand loss experienced through me; he had not lost anything tangible. He was, however, supportive through our diagnosis and prognosis; he agreed to being tested, he was willing to attend appointments with me, he would counsel with me about decisions we had to make, and he did not complain about paying the bills.

As you and your spouse discuss your feelings about infertility, you may find that you share similar perspectives as my husband and me. Open, honest, and respectful discussion, however, can be the key to unlocking and understanding each other more completely. Once you begin to understand how infertility is affecting your spouse, your ability to be productive, supportive, and compassionate will increase. A whole new way to comfort one another may even come into view.

In the case where male factor infertility is involved, the husband's emotions are affected differently. When a man finds out that he cannot reproduce, he may feel that his manhood and masculinity are compromised and it disrupts not only his intimacy but other aspects of his life as well. Dr. William D. Petok said that "men are be susceptible to thinking that they are 'useless' to a partner unless they can make her pregnant."[7] It is common for depression, withdrawal, and sexual desire and dysfunction to be the result of feeling like a failure to his wife.

Learning from Others

The following narratives are the stories and experiences of men who have been involved with infertility. I hope that through their thoughts you will be given the ability to see that there are others who are walking the same path as you. I appreciate each of these men and celebrate their willingness to share some private feelings in their own words. May they be of benefit to you.

JOEL AND KERSTIN

Long before we decided to start a family, I knew that there was a possibility that we would have fertility problems. I was aware of my wife's medical history, and therefore had time to prepare myself for whatever came. As a result, I think I had an easier time dealing with the news about our infertility, as it wasn't so much of a surprise. Regardless, I felt a sense of sadness as I considered the potential that we may never have children. As I enjoyed time spent with my parents and siblings, I felt particularly sad when I considered that we might not have children with whom we could share family experiences and develop lasting relationships. I see the happiness that my siblings and friends with children have in spending time together, and I felt that I would be missing something. Certainly, I would still enjoy life if it was just the two of us, but it seems that I would be missing out on something if we couldn't have children.

During these difficult years, I have had time to ponder how Kerstin and I reacted differently to our infertility, and I attribute it to our difference in focus. Growing up, I had always assumed that I would have children in the future, but it wasn't in the forefront of my mind. Rather, my focus was on my education and deciding on a career so that I could support my family. Like many LDS young women, Kerstin grew up with significant emphasis on becoming a mother and raising a family. Kerstin's priority was having children, while for me, it was far less of a priority. I am not saying that I didn't want children; rather, the news of our inability to have children was less of a disruption to me because it wasn't my primary focus. When our infertility started to impact my ingrained priorities and began to cost us increasing amounts of time and money, the loss became much more tangible to me, and I began to feel more frustrated at our inability to conceive. Additionally, I felt great sorrow because of the sadness and loss that our infertility brought to Kerstin. There are few things I want more in this life than for her to be happy. It was difficult to deal with my feelings of being powerless to have any influence on our situation other than going through a few treatments such as artificial insemination and IVF. I felt as though there wasn't anything I could do to solve our problem. I could only love my wife and reassure her that we would do whatever we could to address our infertility, and so that's what I did. I put my arms around her and promised we would get through this together.

In addition to our differences in focus, I think that my education in the life sciences helped me accept our situation. My understanding of the human body on a scientific level made it easier for me to comprehend how some things can go wrong, thus removing much of the mystery of infertility that often plagues couples. I learned that it is not unusual for certain systems in an organism to not function properly, but for the organism to continue living its life with no other problems. I extended this knowledge to our situation—I felt that despite our inability to have children, we could continue living a rewarding life, as it was only one system that was malfunctioning. As a result, I saw these malfunctions as biological deficiencies rather than fatal errors, and was, therefore, able to understand them better. I found much comfort in my understanding of the human body, which made it easier to rejoice at the small victories we experienced in our efforts to understand our infertility.

I am grateful for how our trial of infertility has changed our relationship. During the ups and downs, there have been moments of great frustration as we have had to spend much of our time and money seeking resolution to our fertility problems, to say nothing of the significant emotional investment. Through it all, we have undoubtedly grown closer together as we have learned to deal with difficult situations as a couple. I know that this strength will be invaluable to our marriage as we continue to face our infertility and deal with other difficulties in the future.

The gospel has been critical to me as I have tried to make sense of this trial and as I have found ways of coping. The gospel gives me hope that despite the challenges in this life, the Lord has a plan, and He will provide a way for us to enjoy all of the blessings available in this life. I know that this promise can be mine as long as I am faithful. Of course I don't know if this means that we will have children in this life or the next, but knowing that a way will be provided has been particularly comforting. At the same time, the focus on the family in the Church makes it hard for those of us who have fertility problems, as a family with children is a part of the gospel that we cannot enjoy. There has been a sense of unfairness as we have considered the fact that we cannot participate in this integral part of the gospel. Along with my wife, I have relied much more heavily on Heavenly Father for understanding and faith, which has not always been easy. There have certainly been times in the past where we have had to turn to Him for strength, but dealing with infertility has extended us beyond what we thought we were capable of. We have always been fairly independent and have not wanted to have to rely on others, so we have had to humble ourselves to approach God and ask for help. It has been amazing to see our faith and trust in Him grow, as well as our thoughtfulness in prayer and seeking His guidance. In the end, I have seen powerful blessings come, as we have grown closer together as a couple and closer to the Lord.

JARED AND EMILY

Jared and Emily have been married for six years. They have been through testing, procedures, and many disappointments. At this point, tests have not been able to determine reason or solution for their infertility.

It is hard not to wonder why this particular trial is happening to us. Past priesthood blessings have mentioned children in my future—not necessarily in the immediate future, but children nonetheless. As I am striving to understand how infertility can coexist with these promised blessings, I look to the gospel for direction. Truthfully, the gospel, on its surface, hasn't always made it necessarily easier to deal with the trial of infertility. The mission of the gospel and the goal of our Father in Heaven not only focuses on individual redemption (Moses 1:39) but also, especially in the latest dispensation, focuses on the salvation of families. This mission of our Father in Heaven has led, and rightfully so, to a large focus in church both over the pulpit and in LDS media on the salvation of families, of which children are a large part. In that regard, the gospel and the way it is taught (and interpreted) makes it a little more difficult to personalize, just as it might be with a non-married member.

On the other hand, I have learned that the gospel is a very personal thing. Salvation is an individual goal between each of us and the Savior; we live righteously for the reason of returning back to His presence. The residuals of reaching this goal include being with those you love who also lived righteously, including your family, for all eternity.

In my quest to apply these gospel teachings to my life with infertility, I have learned that being content with what I have has allowed my perspective to change. I reassure myself by telling myself that I didn't marry my future children, but rather, I married my wife. Obviously, I have always had the thought of children and the potential to be a father in my mind, but first and foremost I made promises with my wife and Father in Heaven, promises not contingent upon whether we had children or not. Reminding myself of this helps ease the pain.

In the process of dealing with infertility, I have chosen to allow our experiences to help me draw me closer to my wife. We share a similar attitude and resolve to make sure we enjoy life regardless of whether we ever have children. I believe we have grown closer together emotionally, physically, and spiritually. We have had a lot of time to be together, understand each other better, and simply love life! We share a trial that is unique to us. Sharing something that only we truly know or understand keeps us more bonded together than we may have been otherwise. In other words, it is not my wife's trial or my trial; it is not my infertility or my wife's infertility; it is our infertility, it is our trial—and we have chosen to allow it to bring us closer.

Surprisingly, being given the opportunity to teach and care for the three- and four-year-olds in church every Sunday has been therapeutic. For two hours each week, I have the chance to not only reach out to them and teach them simple and basic values, but also to be taught by them. I originally thought that it would be difficult and that this responsibility would serve as a constant reminder of our inability to have children. On the contrary, it has been refreshing, even considering the erroneous (at least in my case) axiom that "Teaching Primary is a natural form of birth control." (When someone found out at work that I teach the little ones in my ward, the comment was made, "Well, now you'll never have kids.") It certainly isn't a substitute for having my own children, but seeing their faces every Sunday is definitely one of the highlights of my week.

Infertility has brought sorrows into my life that I never anticipated. I have found that one of the greatest sorrows is not being able to raise a child in what I believe would be a comfortable, structured, and loving environment. I find myself questioning why some children are born in dire and clearly unfit circumstances where they seem doomed for failure and disappointment throughout their lives. I know we wouldn't be able to offer a perfect life for children, but seeing mothers with unwanted children makes it that much more difficult to be content without children.

Additional sorrow comes because we do not know the cause of our infertility. In some aspects, I think it would be better to know whether or not there is even a possibility of having children. Perhaps knowing there is no chance for conception would allow us to move on, in a sense, and allow room for closure.

Sporadic and usually unintentional and non-malignant comments can complicate the healing process and remind me of the sorrow of our infertility. I can go days or even weeks sometimes without thinking about our challenge, but little reminders here and there remind me and reopen wounds. I would say that one of the most frustrating or difficult things has been dealing with comments at my place of employment. Over the last two years, five babies have been born in our relatively small office. These births aren't an issue. The issue arises when the inevitable question is posed, "Jared, don't you want one of these?" or "When are you going to have one of these?" The implication is that I am missing a great deal on eBay or something. Usually I deflect the comments with, "Of course" or "Looks like I'm falling behind." The topic of my childlessness is addressed almost every time someone's child is brought into the office or when an office baby shower is thrown, the former happening at least every two or three weeks. I can understand that someone might pose the question once; however, it usually happens multiple times from the same people. Others in the office automatically assume that we have simply chosen to postpone having children.

I realize that in this forum it's easy for me to point out the ignorant or inappropriate comments made by coworkers, friends, or acquaintances. But I have to ask myself if I would have made similar comments if roles were reversed with some of these individuals. I'd like to think that I would be extremely sensitive and say all the right things at the right times. Perhaps it is a blessing to experience this trial! I do feel that I have become more sensitive to the trials of others even if their trial is not the same as mine.

MATT AND LESLIE

Matt and Leslie were married in 2001. They began their quest for answers to their infertility two years later. After enduring many tests, dead ends, and frustrations, it was determined that they are suffering from male factor infertility.

I have been a member of the Church my whole life, and one of the things that was taught repeatedly was the importance of multiplying and replenishing the earth. Family has always been important to me, especially since I am the youngest of six children. I have always loved kids, thought that I have the ability to bond well with them, and have looked forward to the day that I would have some of my own; my patriarchal blessing even talks about me having kids. Well, my wife and I cannot have children. The fact that we are unable to fulfill this commandment to multiply and replenish the earth leaves me wondering what the deal is—how can I make sense of the promises, the commandments, the blessings, and even the desire for children when they cannot be a part of my life? I am beginning to avoid doing anything with kids since being around kids is just a reminder to me that we do not have any. Seeing what I cannot have just angers me more.

At first when we could not get pregnant, I simply thought it was not the right time and comforted myself by saying that it takes some people longer to have kids. As time went on, we started wondering if there were some issues with our fertility. Honestly, I was really hoping it wasn't me causing the problem; in fact, I was in denial for a long time and was determined that it could not be me and thought my sperm were just fine. I very much wanted it to be a problem with Leslie and not me. I could love her no matter what, even if there was a reason she was unable to have children. But if it were me causing the problem, I wondered if she could still love me.

It was always easier for me to pawn our fertility problems off on Leslie and just watch her go to the doctor. I did not want to endure the tests since the collection process (in order for my sperm to get tested) was far from pleasant. Eventually, I went to be tested, and for a long time it seemed like something always went wrong, and I was unable to provide the sample. Now, that is a great morale booster! Sign me up for more of that! Once my sperm was tested, I faced the shocking news: my sperm was not fine. I felt far from manly! I felt like my manhood had been compromised. It is a definite demoralizer to find out your sperm is not good for what it was meant to do. It is hard for men when male factor infertility is part of the equation, because so much of how society determines manhood and masculinity is based on his ability to procreate. It is easy for a man's sexuality to be affected and for him to feel less of a person.

During these hard times, Leslie was good at finding peace in the gospel. Unlike her, when I was given the bitter cup I took it, drank of it, and became bitter; instead of turning to the Lord, I turned away. I think that our home would be a great place to raise a child, and I have a hard time understanding why the Lord doesn't make it easier so we can do just that. I have seen great blessings in my life with a home, a job to provide for my needs, and no major struggles yet, but why do I have to be the one unable to have children?

I really struggled with Leslie always wanting to talk about our infertility over and over again. All I wanted to do was forget about it, not talk about it, and just let my anger build up. It became obvious pretty quickly that we were dealing with this issue differently. Over time and because I have come to grips with the fact that I am the issue, I have become more willing to talk about it more for her than me.

Everything started to change when I built a home for a urologist. He became a friend, and because I trusted him, I felt comfortable asking him questions. He referred me to the right doctor in his practice that handled cases like mine. Once I chose to be okay with addressing these issues, the ball started rolling. I ended up needing invasive surgery. Yes, I was a little nervous as it was my first major surgery, and it had to do with a very private part of me, but I knew I just had to get over it. Because I was willing to accept this new path and take the often-difficult steps necessary to resolve the problems we were facing, Leslie and I are where we are today—a month away from in vitro. Do I think it is fair that we have to pay over $12,000 to have the blessing of children? No. But at least it is a solution to the problem. I am still angry about the fact we cannot have children on our own, but I have hope that this will work.

As I look back, I wish that Leslie and I had started off by being tested at the same time. If we had, we could have had questions answered sooner and we could have moved toward a solution much faster. Additionally, as I reflect on this trial, I still wonder what I am supposed to learn. I have appreciated that Leslie and I have become closer as husband and wife, but I am still waiting for greater perspective and understanding of why we must suffer in such a way. I know that I should turn to the Lord and rely on Him, but at this point, I am still trying to figure out how to do just that.

PETER AND MICHELLE

Peter and Michelle have been married for nine years. After four rounds of failed artificial inseminations and spending three years seeking medical help in order to have kids, they began to look into adoption. Two years later, through the miracle of adoption, they welcomed their sweet daughter into their home.

Why infertility? Why this trial? My wife and I dealt with this for six and a half years, and my opinion is that the answer is simple: I don't know. I believe that God does intentionally provide people with hard trials—like Job. I believe that trials can be a consequence of sin—like so many other people in the scriptures. But I also believe that most of our trials come simply because we elected in our premortal lives to come to Earth to have a mortal experience. After much prayer, I came to the conclusion that my wife and I were experiencing infertility for that reason: it was just that way. I believe that we deal with infertility because infertility is merely an incident of mortality, no more, and no less. It was one of those trials that came solely because we inhabit a mortal body, and because we were not guaranteed how that body would work or whether it would produce children. I believe that it was an essentially random occurrence that did not contain any inherent meaning. Each individual can and should turn to Heavenly Father to learn for themselves the purpose of their trials.

It might sound nihilistic of me to say that the infertility we experienced was random and had no inherent meaning, but in reality, this way of thinking gave me a great deal of comfort. I felt reassured that Heavenly Father was not mean-spirited or cruel. He loved me enough to create this plan, which I willingly accepted, and trials like infertility were part of that plan. And the fact that it had no inherent meaning did not imply that it was meaningless: it was up to me to figure out what I could learn from it and how I could grow from it. That was so empowering. I have every confidence that people who reach different conclusions about the significance of their infertility will still feel Heavenly Father's love for them—if the reason "it is just part of the plan" can provide me such comfort, surely a concrete reason can provide immeasurable relief to another.

Infertility—specifically, infertility as it pertains to men—is hard for me to write about. To me, it has spiritual connotations, and I am not qualified to speak universally or authoritatively on God's doctrine or the meaning behind trials, nor would I ever try. I am also not qualified to speak in "universals" (infertility is always this, infertility is always that) having experienced infertility only in my own family. I share my thoughts only to suggest that I understand. I hope that level of understanding lends me some credibility when I suggest that I feel there is a way to grapple with the feelings associated with infertility. The way I discovered was not easy, but perhaps something in the following experiences can be helpful to you.

Allow joy to enter your life. I have heard infertility discussed as a grieving process; some grieve for dead children, others grieve for children they have never had. I think that the grieving process is healthy and normal. But as with all grieving processes, there comes a time when it must come to an end. We will likely carry some sadness with us the rest of our lives, but at some point, we must rise from the sackcloth and ashes, regardless of the sadness. I remember reaching a point where I was angry with my friends because they kept having children, and I didn't even have one. It was then when I realized that my healthy grieving had turned into something else entirely. I was being honest with myself; I didn't pretend that nothing was wrong. But at the same time, I was denying myself a joy of life that really had nothing to do with the struggles of my wife and I—one of the great joys of having friends is to rejoice in their blessings—and I realized that I could be happier in the ways that I could control just by deciding that I would. To overcome destructive grief and to find joy, I had to, and did, make a conscious choice to move on.

In other words, I have learned that it is okay to derive enjoyment from life even though you cannot have children. One's quest for enjoyment should not replace proper priorities or even the desire to have children. But, if those priorities are being met, take a trip once in a while. Go on dates with your wife. Hang out with your friends—even (and perhaps especially) with those who have children. In the grand scheme of things, infertility is like having uncomfortable shoes—it might hurt a little more to run in the human race, but you can still run it if you want to badly enough.

There are differences between male and female responses to infertility. Because infertility impacts men differently, men deal with it differently. Women need to talk about it. Regardless of whether men need to talk about it, they don't. There is no universally accepted manly way to talk with your buddies about infertility, especially the biological aspects and most especially the emotional aspects, which every man must eventually deal with in some way or another. There is also no universally accepted manly way to tell your buddies that you are sad because your wife is sad, that you are discouraged, and that you feel like they are moving on with life when you are not. Women cry with each other all the time, but not all guys can or will respond emotionally in the same way. Personally, I did most everything in my power to avoid discussing my feelings regarding our infertility, and still do. Of course, I don't know if that was the best approach or not, but I was true to myself, and although that is a pretty overrated standard of behavior when your sense of self is in such flux, I think it is okay to grant yourself a few luxuries.

Despite all the differences, I believe that men and women grapple with the same cosmic questions: Why can't we accomplish this righteous purpose? Why can people who don't even want kids have them, and we cannot? Don't we have enough faith? Is God listening? Is this God's fault? Is it our fault? At times I felt a little melodramatic telling my wife that I doubted the universe and my place in it. But that was how I felt, at least sometimes. Not having children is a trial, but the internal thoughts, feelings, questions, and doubts are the real struggles of infertility.

Faith is deeper than we comprehend. In my opinion, faith is not simply asking Heavenly Father for something over and over again, believing that He will give it to me because it is a righteous goal and I really want it. Nobody wanted children more than my wife, who to this day has never given birth. Does that mean we are without faith? Of course not. Faith is learning, understanding, and accepting God's will, even if we don't get what we want. It is an understanding that, although we may not understand what is happening to us, we do know that Heavenly Father knows, that He loves us, and that He is aware of what is best for us. On one level, this is scary—we are putting ourselves in the hands of someone who allowed us to deal with this horrible trial. What more horrors could He have in store for us? But on another, more meaningful level, this is the Heavenly Father who wants us to come live with Him again. He knows what is best, and although it may hurt, He will bring us home. I sincerely believe that what I presently feel and know about Heavenly Father, all of which is good and positive, came from my experiences with infertility.

Empathy is a result of trial. A trial like infertility does wonders for one's ability to empathize, which is a blessing I have seen in my life.

Although I am not perfect, I feel like I can now understand others' trials better than before. If you are given the special blessing to learn what it feels like to be on the outside looking in, do not waste that insight. Remember that feeling and put it into action!

Finally, I have learned that blessings come in ways you might not expect. When we adopted our daughter, I felt—and still feel, even more strongly than ever—that she was the child we would have had if we could have naturally conceived a child. For reasons known to Heavenly Father, she just came in a different way. Even if that blessing had never come (but I'm glad it did), I know that Heavenly Father can and will take care of us in so many ways.

Because of the numerous causes of infertility piled on top of individual reactions, it is difficult to represent every situation in just a few pages of a book. I appreciate, however, that each of these men pondered and shared some personal and difficult feelings. You may not experience the exact feelings of Joel, Jared, Matt, or Peter since infertility will affect you differently, but in the end, I hope their words help make sense of your feelings, help verbalize thoughts that have been milling around in your mind, and ultimately help make your emotions more tangible. Perhaps then those emotions will be easier to handle and to share.

Learning from the Scriptures

There are two final things I want to share with you: two examples of male responses to infertility found in the scriptures. I think we learn some powerful lessons from Abraham and Isaac, a father and son who both endured years of being barren.

Let's first consider the story of Abraham. We have already addressed the fact that Abraham was promised "that he might become the father of many nations" (Romans 4:18). I can imagine that this promise, while somewhat overwhelming, was something Abraham looked forward to, felt honored to be his, and held onto with hope in the face of adversity. Over time, Abraham and Sarah recognized that months were turning into decades, and they were still without any indication that this promise of seed was actually going to be fulfilled. Clearly, there was something wrong. Do you think Abraham ever said "This barren wife of mine is dragging me down and keeping me from these blessings?" Or do you suppose he ever had the thought, "My wife is so emotional. Why can't she get control of her feelings? Why do we have to go through this whole saga of disappointment every month?" Of course the scriptures do not contain every detail of the situation, but what they do contain shows that this husband and wife were unified—unified in their sorrow and unified in their rejoicing when, in their old age, they found out they had conceived. We do not see Abraham abandoning Sarah and leaving her alone in her sorrow. He endured *with* her. He was sorrowful that the promise of seed was not being realized. In the face of great adversity, Abraham "staggered (Greek for doubted, hesitated) not at the promise of God through unbelief; but was strong in faith, giving glory to God; And being fully persuaded that, what he had promised, he was able also to perform" (Romans 4:20–21). Abraham exercised remarkable faith, had abiding hope, and remained faithful to the Lord.

Every husband can be just like Abraham. You can give all your energy to your wife by supporting her, being by her side, and being equally committed to the quest for posterity. Pledge that even in the face of the greatest sorrow, you will be ever present with her, physically, spiritually, and emotionally. And despite the challenges and disappointments you face, prove yourself faithful to the Lord through this adversity. Trust in Him. Rely on Him. Know that He is aware of you and wants you to find happiness. The promise and hope of posterity did not end with Abraham. It has, in fact, carried on throughout the generations. You too can hold on to the promise of being blessed with eternal increase and being a father of many nations (see D&C 132:30–31). Do not be staggered, but be filled with hope and faith.

Isaac's wife, Rebekah, was chosen for him by his father's servant. This arranged marriage was a great success because Isaac truly loved Rebekah. There was sorrow to be had, however, when Rebekah found that she was barren and remained barren for twenty years. The scriptures tell us that Isaac "intreated the Lord for his wife" (Genesis 25:21). I love that image! When I think of infertility, I think of a woman on bended knee pleading with all her energy to grant her greatest desire for children. But in this case, we see a man making a deeply sincere and determined request of the Lord. He petitioned the Lord in behalf of his wife and for himself. He then trusted that the Lord would grant his desire.

In a time of sadness for this biblical couple, Isaac recognized something he could do to improve the situation. He knew of his wife's disappointment and her longing. I imagine that as he witnessed her sadness time after time, he felt he alone could not fulfill Rebekah's desire to be a mother. With certainty, he knew that if he sought the Lord's help, joy was possible for them.

As you "intreat" the Lord for you and your wife, you may not see the fruit that Isaac saw. Regardless, you will see your life filled with strength and greater capacity. You will find that your love and devotion for your wife will be enlarged, you will recognize tangible ways you can improve your circumstances, and you will also find an increased ability to cope and endure.

I wish the Lord's choicest blessings upon you as you move forward diligently, make sense of what you are feeling, and try to be united with your wife in this trial. We, as husbands and wives, can overcome this challenge together, especially as we rely on the help of our Heavenly Father. Through Christ, we can receive strength where we feel so inadequate and disappointed. Additionally, we know that because of Him, all things will be made right, and we will receive all the blessings Heavenly Father has promised us.

Notes

1. See James Borin and Natan Bar-Chama, et al, "The Workup of the Infertile Male", In*focus*, Winter 2003, 5.
2. Ibid., 29.
3. See Pamela Madsen, "Message from the Executive Director," In*focus*, Winter 2003, 2.
4. William D. Petok, "Male Factor Infertility: Its Potential Effect On Sex and Sexuality," In*focus*, Winter 2003, 10.
5. Madsen, "Message From the Executive Director," 2.
6. "The Family: A Proclamation to the World," *Ensign*, Nov. 1995, 102.
7. See Petok, "Male Factor Infertility: Its Potential Effect On Sex and Sexuality," 10.

CONCLUSION

Help Thou Mine Unbelief

Not long ago, I attended the adult session of our stake conference. Although it is spiritually packed, this meeting often seems more relaxed than the general session of stake conference. At this particular session, the more informal format was conducive to the viewing of a five-minute DVD segment produced by the Church. The short clip we viewed was an introduction to a Worldwide Leadership Training Broadcast and contained glimpses of the life of our Savior set to the music "Beautiful Savior" and "I Feel My Savior's Love." We watched Christ walk down the roads of humble villages with the Twelve Apostles, we saw Him accept a butterfly from the loving hands of a child, and we witnessed Him picking up bread dropped from a vendor's basket. We then caught a glimpse of a few of the miracles Christ performed in His brief mortal life.

Two of the miracles that caught my attention were Christ performing the healing of a man blinded from birth and the woman healed as she touched the hem of Christ's robe. These timeless stories provide us with great opportunities for spiritual learning and growth.

We know that the blind man had been blind from birth (see John 9:1). Undoubtedly, Christ knew of this man's infirmity and the limitations, struggle, and sadness it caused. In this particular story, the disciples asked Christ,

> Master, who did sin, this man, or his parents, that he was born blind?

Jesus answered, Neither hath this man sinned, nor his parents: but that the works of God should be made manifest in him.

When he had thus spoken, he spat on the ground, and made clay of the spittle, and he anointed the eyes of the blind man with the clay,

And said unto him, Go, wash in the pool of Siloam. . . . He went his way therefore, and washed, and came seeing. (John 9:2–3, 6–7)

There were people in the area who knew this man and were aware of his blindness. After the miracle, when they learned that he could see, they questioned the man: "How were thine eyes opened? He answered and said, A man that is called Jesus made clay, and anointed mine eyes, and said unto me, Go to the pool of Siloam, and wash: and I went and washed, and I received sight" (John 9:10–11). He recounted his story to the Pharisees, who did not believe him. He then testified of the truthfulness of what happened by saying, "One thing I know, that, whereas I was blind, now I see" (John 9:25). Christ's compassion and the will of our Heavenly Father, combined with the faith and obedience of this aged man, produced a miracle.

I remember when the story of the woman touching Christ's robe became one of my favorite New Testament stories (see Matthew 9:20–22, Mark 5:25–34, and Luke 8:43–48). I was a student at Brigham Young University. My husband and I were walking up the east stairs in the Wilkinson Center, and I saw ahead of me a large painting of a woman touching the hem of Christ's robe. My husband and I were in awe at the beauty of the painting (it actually caused us to pause and look at it), and, at that moment, I committed myself to rereading the story so beautifully represented by the artist. Once I had read the story, the painting became more exquisite, and I realized that the immensity of the painting truly mirrored the immensity and power of the miracle.

This woman had suffered for twelve years from an issue of blood. An issue of blood is Greek for hemorrhage (see footnote a to Matthew 9:20). Although I do not know the details of her situation, I surely cannot imagine bleeding for twelve years. The scriptures indicate that she "had spent all her living upon physicians" (Luke 8:43), she had tried everything these physicians had suggested, "and was nothing bettered, but rather grew worse" (Mark 5:26). I would assume that she was in despair and greatly discouraged not only for her health, but for her financial situation and social standing as well. After all, she was considered unclean because of her condition.

But this woman had uncompromised faith. She knew of Christ. She *knew* that He could heal her, "for she said within herself, If I may but touch his garment, I shall be whole" (Matthew 9:21). She went to where she knew Christ would be and, as He passed her, this woman reached out in faith and touched the hem of His robe. The scriptures say that "immediately" (Luke 8:44) and "straightway the fountain of her blood was dried up; and she felt in her body that she was healed of that plague" (Mark 5:29). The story does not end there. When she touched Christ's garment, He knew it, for He "immediately [knew] in himself that virtue had gone out of him" (Mark 5:30). According to the footnote, "virtue" in this verse means power or strength. He turned, looking around to see if He could identify the one who touched Him. When He asked the multitude who had touched Him, His disciples answered Him, perhaps with a bit of sarcasm, "Thou seest the multitude thronging thee, and sayest thou, Who touched me?" (Mark 5:31). It was probably not uncommon for Christ to be touched as He walked through crowds, but this touch was different. The fact that someone had enough faith to cause a miracle in this fashion was most likely uncommon. When His eyes met those of the woman, she "fearing and trembling, knowing what was done in her, came and fell down before him, and told him all the truth.

"And he said unto her, Daughter, thy faith hath made thee whole; go in peace, and be whole" (Mark 5:33–34). It was this woman's faith in the power of God that brought much needed and anticipated healing.

In studying these two stories, my heart was touched by feelings of love for this Man, the Healer. After an exhibition of faith by these common people who had been sorely afflicted for many years, Christ healed them, changing their lives forever.

So what does this mean? The man was blind, the woman was hemorrhaging—that has nothing to do with my inability to have children. But wait. Yes, it does. I truly believe that *if* we allow Him, He too can produce life-altering changes in *our* lives. Let's make the connections together.

With the blind man healed by the hand of Christ, one thing we learn is that he acted as a witness of Christ by testifying of His healing power. Following the miracle, the blind man stood as Christ's witness by testifying boldly of the source of his healing. I am sure this man felt inconvenienced by his limitation of sight. He probably felt uanble to become what he felt he should or what he was meant to become. By restoring his sight through a miracle, Christ enabled this man to testify to the Pharisees and to others of Christ's divinity, thus "the works of God [had been] made manifest in him" (John 9:3). With Christ, we can overcome our limitations and fulfill the tasks we are meant to accomplish. Additionally, as we recognize miracles in our lives, performed by the hand of Christ, large or small, expected or unexpected, we must also be witnesses by bearing a powerful testimony of His ability to heal, comfort, and save us. As an applicable side note, when the Nephites were under bitter affliction, Christ explained to the people of Alma, "I will also ease the burdens which are put upon your shoulders, that even you cannot feel them upon your backs, even while you are in bondage; and *this will I do that ye may stand as witnesses for me hereafter*, and that ye may know of a surety that I, the Lord God, do visit my people in their afflictions" (Mosiah 24:14, emphasis added).

What else can we learn from this blind man? We learn that physical ailments are not caused by sin. The fact that we are barren does not mean that we have done something wrong. That knowledge brings me great comfort. However, what we do with the physical ailment can lead to sin. Are we going to allow the power of Christ to heal our wounded hearts, or are we going to allow the power of Satan to lull us into deep resentment and despair? It is a conscious choice.

Finally, the blind man's miracle teaches that we must be obedient to what Christ asks of us. If someone told me that clay on my eyes and washing in a specific body of water would restore my sight, would I do it? We are told to follow the promptings of the Spirit even if the prompting is far from what we expect. If we are going to ask for the hand of God to change our lives, we must be willing to listen for the answer, follow with faith, and then allow grace into our hearts. Have you heard of grace? According to the Bible Dictionary, grace is "an enabling power." It gives us "strength and assistance." It comes "*after* [we] have expended [our] own best efforts." However, "grace cannot suffice without total effort on the part of the recipient."[1]

Grace is a gift provided by the Savior through His extraordinary Atonement. The blind man had done all that he could have done to fix his eyesight. His limitation could be made right only by the grace of God—the power of Christ. With infertility, we must do everything in our power, being guided by the Spirit, and then invite the power of Christ—the grace of God—to fill in where we lack. Just as we learn in 1 Nephi 3:7, we must "*go* and *do* . . . [and] he shall prepare a way" for us to accomplish the very commandments He gives us (emphasis added).

Let us again consider the miracle of the woman with the issue of blood. She had faith. What does it really mean to have faith? Once again, the Bible Dictionary provides clarification: "To have faith is to have confidence in something or someone. . . . Strong faith is developed by obedience to the gospel of Jesus Christ."[2] Do we have confidence in Christ? Is it confidence without reservation? Are we obedient to the gospel of Jesus Christ? This means going to Church (and actively participating), fulfilling callings with compassion and love, taking upon us the name of Christ in all that we say and do, attending the temple, and more. The immensity of our faith is determined by the intensity with which we do the things we have been commanded to do. Faith is an action. Faith is a choice.

Another thing we learn from this faithful woman is that she tried everything. She exhausted her resources. She went to numerous physicians, perhaps specialists of her time, to find answers, and still nothing. From the words we read, it sounds as though she spent all that she had—for she had nothing left. Does that mean that we should spend everything we have on fertility treatments? Perhaps not. But it does mean that sometimes we are asked to make sacrifices, even financial sacrifices, to accomplish the thing that we have been commanded. For each couple and situation, this will be different; therefore, husbands and wives should counsel with the Lord.

Not only did Christ heal this woman, He granted her comfort and peace. "Christ is the Great Physician who rose from the dead 'with healing in his wings' (2 Nephi 25:13)."[3]

Have you personally reached out, with faith, to touch the hem of Christ's robe? Do you believe He can heal your infirmities and your broken heart? I know He can. That is His role as the Redeemer.

In addition to the timeless stories from the scriptures, the writings of latter-day prophets or other Church leaders can be helpful as we deal with the affects of infertility. If I could publish the talk "Patience" by Elder Neal A. Maxwell given at BYU on November 27, 1979, in this book, I would. It is phenomenal. I could do the same with Elder David E. Sorensen's talk "Faith Is the Answer" from the April 2005 conference. The same could be done with countless other talks. Are these talks directed to the infertile couples of the Church? No, but the power of their words can touch the pained heart of anyone.

So, you might ask, "If I do everything the scriptures say, everything the prophet counsels, and pray with all my soul, will I be guaranteed a child?" It may seem that I am suggesting a formula for guaranteed conception, but it is not that easy. I wish it were. I would like to quote Elder David E. Sorensen because he offers wonderful counsel for this very question:

> The scriptures have many examples of people who were saved after showing great faith. . . . But the scriptures also have many examples of devout people who did not get divine intervention during a crisis. . . . To do well does not mean everything will always turn out well. The key is to remember that faith and obedience are still the answers—even when things go wrong, perhaps especially when things go wrong.
>
> Remember the Lord has promised that He will help us as we face adversity. He has particular compassion for those who suffer. . . .
>
> As part of the Atonement, our Savior suffered all things. He knows physical and emotional pain; He knows the sorrow of loss and betrayal. . . . The world sees peace as the absence of conflict or pain, but Jesus offers us solace despite our suffering. His life was not free of conflict or pain, but it was free of fear and full of meaning.[4]

Faith does not guarantee the results we want or feel we have been promised. Faith does, however, guarantee an increased capacity to endure that which we are asked to experience. Sometimes in the darkness of doubt and in the sadness of sorrow, it *is* hard to believe. It is hard to understand why we must endure such deep disappointment, but that is why He is there. We must believe that all things are possible through Him, and say, "Lord, I believe; help thou mine unbelief" (Mark 9:24). Through His perfect grace, He will make our faith perfect.

I believe that through the strength of Jesus Christ and His infinitely virtuous Atonement, I may come to accept this great suffering, sorrow, and sickness which I have been asked to endure. I know He loves me and is mindful of me individually. I appreciate that He knows my potential, what I can become, and is willing to help me achieve that. I know that as I righteously do all that I can, even with "unwearyingness" (Helaman 10:4–5), Christ will make everything right.

Additionally, I hope you will find peace in the words of the Prophet Joseph Smith as he endured great suffering in Liberty Jail, I know I do, "Let us cheerfully do all things that lie in our power; and then may we stand still, with the utmost assurance, to see the salvation of God, and for his arm to be revealed" (D&C 123:17). I am grateful for moments in my life when His arm has been revealed in small, yet significant ways. I have begun to see each blessing as evidence of His love for and awareness of me. Interim blessings have, indeed, illuminated my life by providing hope in the greatest despair. They have fortified my spiritual energy so that my steps forward can be made with more faith and trust. It is my sincere desire that I will cheerfully do all that is in my power and that I will continue faithful to the end of this trial. May you do the same.

Notes

1. "Grace," Bible Dictionary, 697, italics added.
2. "Faith," Bible Dictionary, 669.
3. James E. Faust, "Strengthening the Inner Self," *Ensign*, Feb. 2003, 5.
4. David E. Sorensen, "Faith is the Answer," *Ensign*, May 2005, 73.

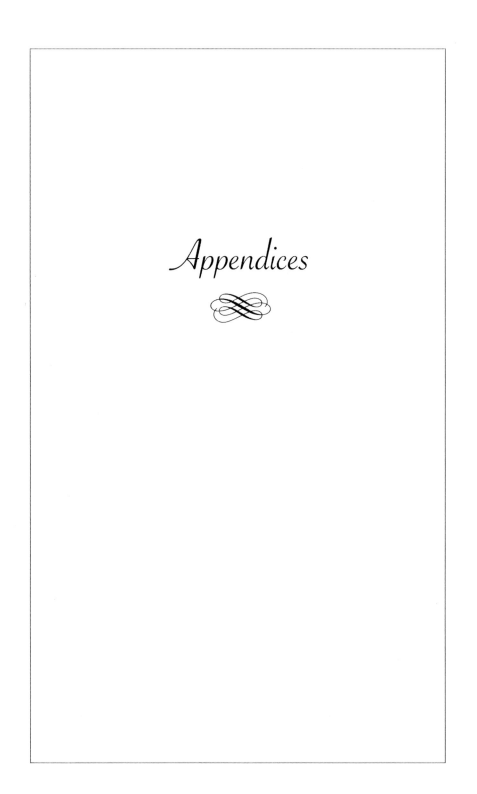

Appendices

APPENDIX A

Supporting Someone Who Has Fertility Challenges

After two years of being unsuccessful at conceiving, my friend finally accepted that she may be infertile. Seeking help to repair her broken heart and realign her confused mind, she explained her situation to her mother. Her mother spoke with great wisdom, saying "The things we want most don't always come right away." Her mother then told her a little secret: children did not come easily for her either. My friend was dumbfounded by the comment since she knew that her mom was pregnant within a year of being married! To my friend and most infertile couples, a year without children could hardly be classified as having difficulty getting pregnant.

As I prepared to share my feelings about infertility with my own mother, I remember wondering exactly how she would be able to relate. After all, my mom and dad began their family with my older sister who came nine months after they were married and had seven children in thirteen years. I knew that she could not empathize, but I also knew that she sincerely wanted to understand. I realized that I could choose to be angry that her ease of having children did not qualify her to adequately comfort me. Or I could choose to play a pivotal role in teaching her about this sorrow that was unknown to her.

This appendix is written to the mothers, fathers, siblings, and friends of those who experience infertility; it is written to those who are fertile. It is intended to provide a new perspective for those who would like to support, help, or understand their loved ones, but who may feel awkward or inadequate in doing so. As you may have already noticed, infertility is a subject that is hard to address with people because of the sensitive nature of the topic and because of the emotion involved. Being informed and prepared may improve your success as you interact with your loved ones. You certainly have the ability to help bear the burden, to offer comfort, and to strengthen those who have cause to suffer.

At baptism, we as members of the Church covenant to be "willing to bear one another's burdens, that they may be light; . . . willing to mourn with those that mourn; . . . and comfort those that stand in need of comfort" (Mosiah 18:8–9). Your willingness and ability to help bear the burden of infertility will make the pain more bearable and the sorrow not so deep. Are you spiritually equipped to bear the burdens of a woman who feels she cannot measure up to other women because she cannot conceive? Do you know what will be required of you as you lift the heavy burden of a husband who feels he has let his wife down because he cannot "multiply and replenish the earth"? Here are some things to consider.

The gospel is family-oriented, as it should be, but it is often hard for a couple dealing with infertility to be reminded of it so often. We find joy in our relationships with those we love and feel comforted that family relationships continue eternally. It is important to remember that families are not just moms and dads with children. A family can be just a husband and wife. A family begins with a husband and wife. A family continues through the experiences of life whether there are no children, one child, or ten children. Children grow up and move on to lives of their own, leaving the core family behind—husband and wife. The husband and wife relationship is at the center of family life. Make sure that, in cases of infertility, you help couples feel that they are a legitimate family.

Be genuine. Don't fake it. If you fake it, they will know. Are you asking them questions about their infertility because you are curious, because you have stewardship over the couple, or because you heard from someone else about their infertility? Or are you asking them questions because you are concerned about them and want to offer your support? What will do you do with the information you gather? Remember that a truly genuine friend asks questions out of deep concern and love. A genuine friend will offer support and strength no matter what happens. This friend will carefully guard the information gathered and will respect the couple's wishes of who they want to know. Provide them with a trusted friend. They are more likely to share with someone they trust.